Captives

Catherine Kenny was born in Brisbane in 1962. She has an Arts/Law degree with honours in History and Law from the University of Queensland, and is currently a solicitor working as a publications officer with the Continuing Legal Education department of the Queensland Law Society. She is interested in oral history and interviewed many of the nurses and collected photographs, diaries and letters from various sources as well as from the women themselves in researching this book.

Captives

Australian Army Nurses in Japanese Prison Camps

Catherine Kenny

University of Queensland Press

First published 1986 by University of Queensland Press,
Box 42, St Lucia, Queensland, Australia
Reprinted 1989

Typeset by University of Queensland Press
Printed in Australia by The Book Printer, Melbourne

Distributed in the USA and Canada by
International Specialized Book Services, Inc.,
5602 N.E. Hassalo Street, Portland, Oregon 97213-3640

Cataloguing in Publication Data
National Library of Australia

Kenny, Catherine, 1962-   .
    Captives: Australian army nurses in Japanese prison
    camps.

    Bibliography.
    Includes index.

    1. World War, 1939-45 — Prisoners and prisons,
    Japanese. 2. Military nursing — Australia — History —
    20th century. 3. Australia. Army. Australian Army
    Nursing Service. I. Title.

940.54'72'52

ISBN 0 7022 1926 6

In memory of my late father
Maxwell Gordon Kenny, AM, RFD, ED

Contents

Foreword

When invited to write the foreword to this work, I was naturally delighted. Reading the author's B.A. Honours thesis, "Australian Army Nurses in Japanese Captivity 1942–1945", I felt privileged to be associated with a young Australian who has the ability, sensitivity and perception that Catherine Kenny has so clearly displayed.

The amount of research that has so evidently been involved is quite staggering. Sorting the information gained and putting it all together in story form was an even greater task. The end result is this authentic, sensitive and historical work — a book that I would like to think will reach the shelves of every municipal and school library.

On our release after those years of captivity under appalling conditions and our return to Australia and our families, our experiences were still vivid in our minds. We were still grieving over the loss of so many dear friends and colleagues and bitterly resentful of the waste of so many young lives — young Australian women who possessed the skills and knowledge to contribute so much to the community and to humanity.

Such feelings and experiences could not immediately be put into words or recounted.

Now, forty-one years later, Time the Healer and the increasing interest of the younger generation of Australians prompt us to speak more freely of those distressful days.

It is noteworthy that there has never previously been an account written of the trauma, humiliation and intimidation suffered by the six Army nurses and their administrative and missionary colleagues who were taken prisoner in Rabaul and later transferred to Japan and imprisoned there for the balance of the war.

We are indeed indebted to Catherine Kenny for her most valuable contribution to the history of Australian Army nurses in Japanese captivity during World War II.

Vivian Statham (née Bullwinkel)
Perth, April 1986

Preface

Most of the members of the Australian Army Nursing Service (AANS) who served during World War II underwent challenging experiences, but some nurses became prisoners of the Japanese, thirty-two on Banka Island and Sumatra and six in Rabaul and Japan. They experienced personal deprivation that was unique in their lives and in the history of the AANS. Unexpectedly captured by an enemy they knew little about, they underwent a rapid period of adjustment and then years of adaption to a life which had few of the traditional supports. The treatment meted out by individual Japanese differed, but on the whole both groups suffered from a shortage of food, in some cases lack of water, little medication, few comforts, no male assistance and separation from family and friends; and yet the majority survived.

Both groups developed survival techniques and more importantly formed strong bonds of loyalty and identity. The military status of these women established them as an easily identifiable group of females interned during the war. For their part they revealed a consciousness of themselves as Australians, nurses and, less obviously over the years of captivity, as military personnel. They were foremost members of a community, but these three factors affected their outlook in varying degrees. They were certain of their loyalties and, secure in that position, they effectively bolstered each other when hope was essential for survival.

All the nurses accepted the responsibility of acting as a group and were wholehearted in their support for each other. Their response to deprivation was a positive adaption to circumstances. As they sailed optimistically out of Sydney Harbour in February 1941 they could not have contemplated the future that lay before them.

This story is a chronological narrative of the wartime experiences of these women. It is not designed to be an analytical and academic work, or an accusation against Japan; no nation is above reproach in wartime. Any scholar wishing to do further research should consult my thesis, *Australian Army Nurses in Japanese Captivity 1942–1945*, held at the History Department, University of Queensland, for further documentation and footnotes and an extensive bibliography.

Few other works exist on this topic. The women themselves have little in the way of personal records, for during captivity it was difficult to keep written material. The Japanese periodically searched for diaries and there were severe consequences for those who kept them. In Japan there were diary inspections every three to four months, so diaries were carefully hidden or thrown down the lavatory. Miss Betty Jeffrey kept her diary sewn inside a small pillow for much of the time. The women got to know the habits of the guards; if the search was for cigarettes, the written matter would normally be ignored. Sylvia Muir, now Mrs McGregor, kept her drawings in a prominent position so there was no suspicion. After the nurses in Sumatra were rescued and were recuperating in Singapore, they were asked by Army authorities to hand over their belongings for what they thought was fumigation, but all the material was destroyed. Diaries, notes, music and recipe books carefully hidden during captivity were lost. Some had refused to part with these treasures and now the Australian War Memorial has an increasing collection.

I would like to thank all those who assisted me in this work. I am deeply indebted to those Army nurses who were prisoners of war and who took part in my research; a number of personal items were kindly lent to me and assistance was given when many would rather have forgotten. Thanks are due to members of the staff of the Australian War Memorial, Canberra, and sections of the Australian Archives Offices in Canberra and Melbourne, the staff of Central Army Records Office, Melbourne and Chancery House (Army Archives), Melbourne. I would also like to thank members of the History Department at the University of Queensland, especially Professor M. Thomis who first recognized the potential in my research and suggested I should have it published. The patience of the staff of the University of Queensland Press and those who helped edit and proofread must also be acknowledged.

Finally, I would like to thank my mother whose support and help through my Honours year and thereafter in the production of this book was invaluable. This book is for both my parents.

Catherine Kenny

"The Best of our Young Nation's Womanhood"

On 4 February 1941, a year and a half after Australian Prime Minister Robert Menzies declared Australia at war with Germany, the *Queen Mary*, the *Aquitania* and the Dutch liner the *Nieuw Amsterdam* left Sydney harbour to deafening cheers, bands, foghorns, sirens and singing of the "Maori Farewell".

On board the *Queen Mary* were fifty-one Australian Army nurses and nearly six thousand troops, "Elbow Force", most of whom thought they were heading for the Middle East, where the majority of Australian troops were stationed. A day out of Fremantle, on 13 February, those on the *Queen Mary* were told their destination was Malaya. The announcement generated disappointment, anger and frustration amongst the 8th Division, including the nurses. Sister Ellen M. Hannah wrote soon after, "We were all disappointed when we were sent to Malaya, but who knows we may go further afield yet." The "never to be forgotten sight" of the *Queen Mary* forging away from the rest of the convoy, to the accompaniment of cheers and rousing music, was symbolic of Australia's divided responsibilities. There was no indication of the dramatic defeats to be suffered or the horrors ahead for those who became prisoners of war a year later.

The 22nd Brigade and attached units that left Australia on this occasion were part of the 8th Division Australian Imperial Force. Sent to Malaya under the command of Major-General H. Gordon Bennett, this Australian force retained its individual identity, rather than being incorporated within the British force. It was equipped with a wide range of ancillary services including medical, dental and nursing staff, postal units, pay officers, provost companies and supply depots. Of the Australian Army nurses on board the *Queen Mary*, forty-three were carefully chosen for the 2/10th Australian General Hospital (AGH) and another eight for the 2/4th Casualty Clearing Station (CCS); as well there were three masseurs, or physiotherapists.

Like the young men who flocked to join the Army, nurses from the civilian community and the dormant Australian Army Nursing Service (AANS) Reserve eagerly enlisted for service in Australia or abroad, once war was declared. The thousands of nurses who volunteered far exceeded the needs of the service. Those who served during World War II numbered 3477 in all. To be eligible the candidate had to be a fully qualified nurse, with no less than three years' training in medical and surgical nursing in a hospital. She had to be a British subject domiciled in Australia, between twenty-five and thirty-five years of age and single, widowed or divorced without dependants.

The same standards of general health were required as for male recruits, although there was no special height or chest measurement! The principal matrons of the military commands and the senior members of the profession who selected the recruits were allowed some discretion: "Good character with personal attributes essential to the making of an efficient member of the AANS."[1] The main duties of the nurses were to care for the sick and wounded troops and sick and injured servicewomen.

Despite the exacting standards required to enter the AANS, the nurses who left with "Elbow Force" in February had little military experience. The 2/10th AGH had been hastily formed and temporarily established in the Sydney showground, with staff from all over Australia under the command of Colonel E.R. White. The difficulties of adjusting to military procedure were quickly overcome during the ensuing voyage. The nurses under Matron Olive D. Paschke undertook their duties in the ship's hospital, which commenced to function on 2 February 1941, with accommodation for 150 patients. The smoking-room was converted into a ward and the theatre was on a lower deck. The 2/4th CCS ran a dressing station on the sixteenth deck. The total blackout conditions increased the stifling atmosphere as they moved towards the tropics, particularly for the nurses who worked in long-sleeved grey cesarine dresses with starched white collars and cuffs.

Regular free periods and recreation encouraged friendships. Lieutenant-Colonel T. Hamilton, commanding officer of the 2/4th CCS, wrote: "From the first day they joined us aboard the *Queen Mary* [the nurses] picked up the 'esprit de corps' of the unit to an astonishing degree."[2] In the stately, beautifully appointed surroundings of the ship they enjoyed a leisurely cruise. The nurses, reportedly, made a "very pretty sight" dotted along the ship when it arrived in Singapore with troops to strengthen the security of the Empire. The exhilaration of arrival, their confidence and warm welcome were indicative; they felt there was a purpose in their presence.

The siting of the medical units in Malaya lacked any strategic pattern, partly because the 8th Division was held in reserve without an individual role until July 1941, and partly because of the advantage of using malaria-free areas. The 2/10th AGH was established in Malacca in part of the large, relatively modern civil hospital. Its location on top of a hill was unfortunate: at night it was ablaze with lights and, as the Port of Malacca was unsuitable for sea evacuation, lengthy road transport had to be arranged. Nonetheless, it had full facilities for medical and surgical treatment, and large, well-ventilated wards accommodating two hundred beds; in the event of an emergency, sixteen hundred beds were available. The hospital commenced to provide the medical and surgical services for all Australians in Malaya. It dealt mainly with skin complaints, malaria, common colds, accidents and anxiety neuroses, but the number of sick was not excessive.

Initially there was a shortage of medical equipment and supplies. Lieutenant-Colonel J.G. Glyn White, Deputy Assistant Director of Medical Services, Headquarters AIF Malaya, expected the hospital to bring its own equipment and medical supplies, but these were not due for some time. The situation was alleviated with assistance from the civilian hospital, and by using equipment the staff brought with them or had sent from Australia. Staff Nurse Joyce Tweddell wrote, "if it had not been for our own instruments plus the doctors' we would have been in training for our POW days". The nurses used gas refrigerators and unreliable primus stoves instead of sterilizers (as if they were under canvas) and contended with poor drains and a shortage of taps, but these were difficulties that had to be surmounted.

The 2/4th CCS did not have the same permanency as the hospital. The nurses staffed a small 50-bed hospital at Port Dickson but were also moved to Kajang and Johore Bahru, where they acted as a small hospital with 150 to 200 beds, until the 2/13th AGH relieved them in November 1941 and they returned to their unit at Kluang. Their duties were the usual shift hours of a small hospital — nursing (using cut down kerosene tins as sterilizers), teaching orderlies, making dressings, conserving stores and improvising and preserving equipment. The small size of the CCS engendered a strong unit loyalty and pride and the nurses zealously guarded their position.

> Everyone liked the nurses. Hailing from Tasmania, South Australia and Western Australia, they were representative of the best of our young nation's womanhood. Their average age was thirty, and being glamorous had few attractions for them. They were keen to get on with the job for which they had enlisted.[3]

The nurses' professional value in the hospital and CCS was apparent in their care of the patients, management of the wards and in the training they gave to the orderlies. Moreover, the presence of these women raised the morale of their units. The relationships they established during peacetime were invaluable for the efficient treatment of the wounded some nine months later.

The Australian War Cabinet had an ambivalent attitude to the defence of the Far East, influenced by such warnings as the French capitulation in Indo-China and the recommendations of the Singapore Conference that had been held in 1940. Australian interest in defence against Japan largely revolved around protection of Singapore, viewed as the last bastion of British power in the Far East and Australia's first line of defence. Situated at the southern tip of the Malayan Peninsula, Singapore controlled the Straits of Malacca, the main sea lanes of communication between the Far East and Europe.

The Singapore Conference had been held from 22-31 October 1940, attended by staff officers from India, Australia, New Zealand and Burma, with an American naval officer as an observer. All possible Japanese action in the Pacific region had been considered; it was essential to prevent the Japanese from establishing naval and air bases within striking distance of vital points in Malaya, Burma, Netherlands East Indies, Australia and New Zealand. Malaya had inadequate defence resources and the conference decided it was necessary to maintain army and air forces to deal with raids, and naval and air forces in sufficient strength to ensure continuance of vital trade, to protect troop convoys and to carry out other local defence tasks. Singapore's effectiveness as a stronghold of naval power depended on what forces the overcommitted British could spare. The general conclusion recorded by the Australian delegation was that, in the absence of a main fleet in the area, the forces and equipment available for the defence of Malaya were totally inadequate to meet a vigorous Japanese attack. The minimum naval forces needed to safeguard essential commitments in Australian and New Zealand waters could be provided by recalling their forces then serving in other war zones.

The conclusions of the Australian delegation and the views of the Australian Chief of Staff had inspired grave concern in the Australian War Cabinet, but it considered that Indian troops, rather than Australian, should be deployed to rectify the problems in Malaya. In November 1940 it modified its attitude and offered a brigade, together with the necessary maintenance troops and equipment on a limited scale, but on condition that this force would be sent to the Middle East as soon as possible. The British Prime Minister, Winston Churchill, accepted the offer in December, promising that the Australian brigade would be relieved by an equivalent Indian force in May 1941, but expressing the view that a Japanese attack was less likely than it had been after June 1940 when the collapse of France allowed the establishment of Japanese bases in French Indo-China. Despite Churchill's placatory comments, the force that departed in February 1941 remained in Malaya and was reinforced throughout the year, as Japanese aggression became more apparent.

The need to defend Malaya led to the Australian

War Cabinet's decision in February 1941 to retain the 8th Division for service in Australia and the Far East. A number of AIF forces were deployed, including the posting of the 22nd Battalion of the 23rd Brigade in March to Rabaul, capital of the Mandated Territory of New Guinea. A slender chain of the 8th Division forces thus stretched from Malaya to New Guinea.

The eager and appreciative response to the arrival of the nurses in Malaya was not evident in the reception and treatment of six Australian Army nurses detached to part of the 2/10th Field Ambulance at Rabaul, New Britain, to join Major E.C. Palmer, Senior Medical Officer of the force, and Captain S.E.J. Robertson and twenty male orderlies. On 8 April 1941 the six nurses sailed from Sydney on the troopship *Zealandia*, with full winter and summer kit, to an unknown destination. Sister Kathleen (Kay) I.A. Parker, formerly Matron of the Yass District Hospital, was in charge. She had been granted permission to choose her own staff although she was not allowed to know her destination. She chose five staff nurses — a family friend Daisy (Tootie) Keast, an acquaintance she had met at Ingleburn Camp Hospital, Marjory J. Anderson, two of her former staff at the Yass District Hospital, Eileen M. Callaghan and Mavis C. Cullen, and Lorna M. Whyte. They discovered their destination when they arrived in Rabaul on Anzac Day 1941, and found they were the only servicewomen on the island.

On arrival Captain Robertson took them to their cottage but for three weeks they were left to their own devices. Anderson wrote in her diary on 27 April, "All day Sunday was spent feeling very sorry for ourselves". Meals (frequently cold) were brought up in an ambulance or truck but otherwise the medical officers ignored them. The Returned Servicemen's Association, however, supplied them with tables and chairs, a mirror, an icebox and later a refrigerator and a gramophone. This made their previously near-empty quarters at Namanula comfortable, and the local civilians provided more interesting food. The reason for the medical officers' attitude is not clear, but the nurses assumed that they did not enjoy functioning as a small hospital (it was a Field Ambulance) and did not normally have permanent female nursing staff. After repeated representations the nurses were suddenly allowed to work. "The patients who had endured the well-intentioned but sometimes ungentle ministrations of the orderlies were of course delighted to see them."[4] The medical orderlies were also pleased to have the nurses' friendly and efficient presence, but relations with the medical officers were always reserved.

The hospital where they worked on day and night shifts comprised a large tent and several smaller ones on the outskirts of Rabaul, some distance from the nurses' quarters. The medical arrangements under canvas were primitive, and similar improvisations to those of the 2/4th CCS in Malaya had to be employed. Any seriously ill or surgical cases were taken to the European civilian hospital at Namanula, which was almost a military hospital as the administrative staff cared for civilians and military personnel. The eruption of the volcano Matupi spewed scoria and dust from July until October, killing the vegetation, poisoning the hospital's water and rotting the tents and the nurses' clothes. Several new sites were tried and finally the unit moved into Government House, which had been vacated by the Administrator in September. The new site had excellent facilities, and a supply of chlorinated water was arranged by the battalion hygiene service.

Despite their depressing reception and their eventual work activities, there was plenty of time for entertainment and exploration of the tropical island. Like the civilian population they had natives to do their household chores. The civilians extended hospitality but most of the nurses' social life was provided by the officers of the various units and parties were regularly attended. They frequented the Rabaul Hotel and the Cosmopolitan Hotel, were introduced to native customs and visited the surrounding villages. Despite their small number, Army rules still applied, although Sister Parker was understanding of misdemeanours. The beautiful Country Club was out of bounds but the nurses still attended parties there! Non-commissioned officers could not visit their house but Keast would sometimes sit outside and talk to a young soldier she had not previously met, about their mutual hometown, Junee in New South Wales. The Army nurses did not meet socially with the six administrative nurses on the island, who had been established in Rabaul first and had their own friends and responsibilities. Once they began working all the nurses were made to feel very important.

War is Declared

The situation in the Pacific did not stabilize during 1941; reinforcements were sent to Malaya and minimal forces to Rabaul. In July 1941 the AIF in Malaya was given a fixed defence role in the area comprising Johore and Malacca. If the remote possibility of a Japanese attack did eventuate, then Mersing, a fishing village on the east coast of Johore, eighty-four miles northeast of Johore Bahru, was expected to be the point of action. The 2/10th AGH in Malaya was complemented and by November its bed strength had increased to twelve hundred. Stocks of medical supplies were prepared for any eventuality. The expansion of the Australian forces in Malaya necessitated another General Hospital and the 2/13th AGH arrived on 15 September 1941. It had been hastily raised in Southern Command as a six hundred bed hospital for service in Malaya, but it had the advantage of its senior officers' being appointed from existing units already in Malaya. Colonel O.C. Pigdon came from the 2/2nd Convalescent Depot to take command, and Lieutenant-Colonels C.H. Osborn, senior surgeon, and W.A. Bye, senior physician, came from the 2/10th AGH. Matron Irene

M. Drummond was appointed from the 2/4th CCS, where she was replaced by Temporary Matron Kathleen Kinsella. The 2/13th AGH staff departed from Australia on the hospital ship *Wanganella* with fifty-one Army nurses. No duties were required of the nurses on board but some taught basic nursing to the orderlies and stretcher bearers. The staff attended lectures on tropical medicine, and enjoyed the convivial atmosphere.

The 2/13th AGH arrived in Singapore to find they had no hospital. Staff Nurse Jessie Simons recalled, "Once ashore we were amazed that there was no urgent need for us". In November 1941 they took over an unfinished mental hospital at Tampoi, seven miles from Johore Bahru, that consisted of inconveniently scattered low concrete wards with sheltered connections between them. The wards had poor ventilation, but the theatre was adequate and there was sewerage and sufficient water and light. The 2/13th AGH was reputedly the best equipped hospital sent overseas; in reality it suffered the same shortages as the 2/10th AGH. The 2/13th AGH had very little time to organize before the Japanese invaded, but by 8 December the hospital was equipped with 1183 beds, and had benefited from the hard work of the staff and donations of equipment from the Sultan of Johore. In the few weeks before the war the nurses were busy lecturing orderlies on theatre technique, bandaging and nursing, skills which proved vital when the nurses were later evacuated.

The hospitals in Malaya and Rabaul were relatively busy but, until the war threatened them, there was plenty of time for the staff to enjoy the pleasures of the tropics. The 2/10th AGH nurses' quarters were cool and comfortable, and the Red Cross supplied them with sewing machines, material, gramophones, records and books. The nurses were provided with Amahs, female house servants who did their cooking, cleaning, ironing and washing. Staff Nurse Dorothy Sheehan now Mrs Campin, recollected, "We never did anything for ourselves. We had Amahs to do everything for us. We even had ball boys when we played badminton." Matron Paschke was reported in the *Australian Women's Weekly* as saying: "Some days we feel like film stars . . . The local residents send us huge baskets of orchids, presents of fruit, and invitations to their homes or clubs."

The nurses were furious when their role was misconstrued, and felt that letters from home exaggerated their leisurely existence. As honorary members of beautifully appointed European clubs, the nurses enjoyed the marvellous sporting facilities once they had acclimatized. They shopped and became adept at bargaining. Singapore leave was granted and they visited the famous Raffles Hotel, the swimming club, yacht club, nightclubs and the many other entertainments Singapore offered. They visited gold and tin mines, Kuala Lumpur, rubber plantations and scenic sights. Recreation leave was arranged every two months for four days at Fraser's Hill, a delightful mountain resort. One nurse said, "To us the jungle was a matter of interest, not something to be fought and conquered". They were military personnel, however, and as such always wore uniforms, and were only allowed out in pairs or in foursomes with officers. Those disgruntled nurses who broke these rules and fraternized with non-commissioned Army personnel were confined to barracks for a fortnight.

Major-General R.M. Downes, Director-General of Army Medical Services, visiting Malaya in mid-1941, found the nurses' conditions were good. The only cause of complaint was that their clothing and equipment allowance (£40.00 supplemented by £10 from the Australian Red Cross and Australian Comforts Fund) was inadequate. Their unsuitable uniforms (which had been cut off at the elbows) were to be replaced by an open-necked dress designed for the tropics.

To the troops these women represented their mothers, wives, sisters and girlfriends, with whom they could share their experiences and from whom they could receive helpful support when, as men, they seemed to be doing very little. Reinforcements were greeted with a barrage of questions about the latest Australian news and letters were shared, but it was easy to forget, when mail was irregular and papers heavily censored, that there was a military threat and a war on "outside".

This complacent mood was shattered by the Allied defeats. Mrs Jessie Eaton-Lee, formerly Staff Nurse J.J. Blanch, recalled, "We were told by our spies that the Japs all wore glasses and couldn't see at night . . . they weren't supposed to be able to do anything". The Hague Convention No. 3 1907, ratified by Japan and the United States of America, provided that hostilities between the Contracting Powers "must not commence without a previous and explicit warning, in the form of either a declaration of war, giving reasons, or an ultimatum with a conditional declaration of war". Diplomatic relations were continuing when the surprise Japanese attacks took place on American and British territories. On the afternoon of 8 December 1941 the Federal Cabinet unanimously decided that Australia would declare war on the Japanese from 5.00 p.m. that day. On 16 December Major-General Gordon Bennett asked for at least one Australian division from the Middle East, and on 25 December the Australian government sent strong requests to Churchill and Roosevelt (who were conferring in Washington) that Singapore be reinforced. Churchill replied that he did not believe Singapore would fall and defence matters were under control. The Allies, particularly Australia, were now vulnerable to Japanese penetration.

In less than two months the Japanese advanced from Singora to the Straits of Johore. The Australian troops were sandwiched between poorly trained and disorganized Indian troops stationed in Malaya north of Johore and Malacca and the fortress troops defending Singapore and the adjoining area. In marked contrast, well trained and experienced Japanese soldiers landed at Khota Bahru, Patani and Singora. Singapore was bombed. The Australian medical units were extended to their optimum capacity. One nurse remembered, "At last we were to do the job for which we had prepared and waited".

The medical and nursing staff, however, also had to retreat from the Japanese, whose three-pronged attack pressed south along the east coast from Khota Bahru, advanced down the centre of the Peninsula, and poured soldiers towards the west coast where they engaged the forces defending Jitra. The only two Allied battleships, *Prince of Wales* and *Repulse*, were sunk by Japanese aircraft on 10 December 1941. There was inadequate Royal Air Force cover to protect them. This had a sudden disastrous effect on the morale of the 2/10th AGH and the local townspeople. The position of the 2/10th AGH at Malacca became untenable as the Japanese forces worked their way down the west coast until by 4 January 1942 the defensive position was centred on the Slim River.

The hospital set up for emergency action when the fighting began but progressively packed its eight hundred tons of equipment and diverted its patients to the 2/13th AGH. Sister A. Irving commented, "As usual, the imminence of operations was a more potent healer than any other method". Each day Radio Tokyo advised the nurses that the Japanese had no intention of bombing the hospital but just before the withdrawal of the remaining staff it advised them to leave within forty-eight hours or they would be cut off from the main British forces. By 10 January the patients were relocated and the staff were divided between the 2/13th AGH at Tampoi and the 2/4th CCS at Kluang. The day after the unit left, the site at Malacca was heavily bombed. The new site — formerly a boys' school, Oldham Hall, two miles north of Singapore — commenced to function almost as soon as it was opened on 16 January 1942. The school had been hurriedly evacuated and torn books, broken furniture and fittings had to be cleared, walls pulled down and a clean two hundred bed hospital organized under Matron Paschke's supervision.

> Then followed a somewhat hectic period of erecting beds and organizing wards. Patients were arriving almost before the beds were erected. We boiled our instruments in billies on spirit stoves until the engineers equipped us with gas stoves. All available manpower was unpacking equipment and digging trenches. Water was not laid on and had to be carried. The ablution-centre for the up-patients was a quite inadequate and sorry affair.[5]

The hospital rapidly expanded to accommodate over eight hundred people. Bungalows were claimed in the three adjoining streets, Manor House (formerly a boarding house) took the surgical cases, and tents were erected in the grounds of the two main hospital buildings. Men lay everywhere, on stretchers, floors, verandas, garage floors and eventually in grave-like trenches the troops dug. Staff Nurse A. Betty Jeffrey recalled:

> Everyone of the fellows in the beds had what we called his tin hat and if he didn't have a tin hat we put a clean bed pan on him. They looked good too! Those we could get under the beds we'd put under the beds. You had a little bit more protection because it was a wooden building which rattled like mad and all the dust came out of the ceiling.

The hospital lost most of its equipment on trains that were bombed, so necessary supplies were commandeered from other sources. Food rations mainly consisted of bully beef and tinned food although the Red Cross was invaluable with its assistance and supplies. The vulnerability of the Manor House position, supposedly well within the safe perimeter, was exposed when it was shelled; two members of the male staff were killed and others wounded. The damage was not substantial but morale was severely affected.

The 2/13th AGH similarly vacated its position at Tampoi. It had rapidly expanded to a twelve hundred bed hospital when the 2/10th AGH was established near Singapore. The normal time given to move a general hospital was six weeks; the 2/13th AGH moved and reopened in thirty-eight hours. Their new site was St Patrick's School, twenty-five miles away on the southside of Singapore Island, where they had stayed when they first arrived. Staff Nurse Jessie Simons remembered, "A lot of our hospital furniture and equipment was piled up in the school playground by the removers, and we moved in on those piles like a horde of looters, each intent on getting the best for her own department, no matter how. Most undignified, but matron was not about." It was too small for the mounting number of patients who were accommodated in the quartermaster's store, gymnasium and chapel. The wounded were frequently left outside on the lawn until there was room inside. The nurses would bodily protect the men during the raids and used their unopened trunks as barricade walls. Blackout precautions increased difficulties. On 30 January the hospital kitchen and one ward, very close to Allied machine-guns and other weapons, received a direct hit but there were no casualties. On 31 January the causeway between Singapore Island and the mainland was blown.

Throughout the withdrawals the staff worked day and night until they were relieved. Miss Betty Jeffrey recalled that on one occasion she worked from

7.30 a.m. to 10.30 a.m. the next day. Very little sleep was possible because of the continual noise of planes and bombing. There were never less than four raids a day but this was preferred to the periods of ominous silence. Patients came straight from the battlefield with little or no treatment from the Regimental Aid Posts. There were numerous sick malaria patients, some of whom had been badly wounded but had walked for ten to fifteen days without proper footwear. It was difficult to find blood donors who had not had malaria. Invariably the surgical cases arrived at night and theatres worked constantly. Some of the surgeons operated continuously for seventy-two hours. Frequently the nurses were too busy with their patients or too tired to go to the trenches. A nurse remembered, "The general atmosphere, however, was unforgettable, everyone worked hard and happily, petty irritations of earlier days were forgotten, the heat and mosquitoes were no longer annoying and there was a camaraderie everywhere." The 2/4th CCS nurses were moved to safer positions with the hospitals, but returned to their unit whenever possible. The strength and positive presence of the nurses had a marked effect on the morale of patients and staff.

The Australian Army nurses in Rabaul and Malaya were in as much danger as the men themselves. They had been given no defensive training, and remained in vulnerable areas until it was too late for some to escape. The 2/10th AGH and 2/13th AGH were given Air-Raid Precaution training consisting of physical exercises and instructions on the use of gas masks and trenches. At Tampoi part of the wall around the

2/13th AGH was pulled down so the nurses could run into the jungle, but they were given no training on how to survive once they escaped. The six nurses in Rabaul were given marching practice and similar lessons but they refused to cooperate as they considered their task was nursing, not retreating to air-raid shelters.

Once the fighting started all nurses carried their gas masks, tin hats and kits everywhere, and wore Red Cross armbands to indicate they were non-combatants and, as such, protected personnel under the Geneva Red Cross Convention (27 July 1929), which Japan had ratified and which the Japanese Prime Minister, Tojo, agreed to observe on 29 January 1942. Chapter III, Article IX of the convention stated, "The personnel charged exclusively with the removal, transportation, and treatment of the wounded and sick, as well as with the administration of sanitary formations, and the chaplains attached to armies, shall be respected and protected under all circumstances. If they fall into the hands of the enemy they shall not be treated as prisoners of war." Chapter III Article XII stated that unless there was contrary agreement the protected persons were to be returned as soon as possible to the belligerent to whose service they were attached. Staff Nurse Vivian Bullwinkel, now Mrs Statham, recalled that as Colonel Pigdon of the 2/13th AGH issued the armbands he qualified his actions by saying he had little faith in their effectiveness. Major-General Gordon Bennett held a quiet cocktail hour for a few nurses just before Christmas 1941, during which he made a short speech expressing concern for the nurses' safety and emphasized that they were in far greater danger than the sisters who fled Greece in April 1941.

News filtered through to Singapore of the rape and deaths of British nurses by Japanese soldiers in Hong Kong on 25 December 1941. On Christmas morning just after the surrender, St Stephen's College Emergency Hospital, Hong Kong, had been stormed by Japanese soldiers. A Red Cross flag flew over the doorway but the Japanese bayoneted the two senior doctors and some of the patients, and repeatedly raped the nurses over a period of twenty-four hours. Three of these nurses were later killed. An English officer seriously suggested that the 2/13th AGH nurses in Singapore should be shot to escape a similar fate.

Largely due to the efforts of Colonel A.P. Derham, Assistant Director Medical Services 8th Division AIF, the nurses were finally evacuated despite disapproval at command level. Derham was officially responsible for divisional units, but he assumed "moral" control over all matters affecting the medical services, including the nurses about whom he was particularly concerned. He repeatedly recommended to Major-General Gordon Bennett between 20 and 30 January 1942 that the nurses be evacuated on the first possible hospital ship, but this was rejected on the grounds that it would have a bad effect on civilian morale. He made a further appeal on 8 February 1942, supported by Colonel J.R. Broadbent, Assistant Adjutant and Quartermaster-General, but it was also denied. Derham was reminded he was only responsible for divisional units. After the failure of the second appeal he arranged with Lieutenant-Colonel J. Glyn White, Deputy Assistant Director Medical Services (DADMS), 8th Division AIF, that as many nurses as possible were to be evacuated with casualties on the pretext that they were travelling on duty.

On 10 February, six nurses from the 2/10th AGH were given five minutes notice to depart on the hospital ship *Wah Sui*. There were about 350 men on board including 127 AIF sick and wounded for whom the nurses cared during the trip to Batavia. Bully beef and Christmas cake were the principal diet. The ship was painted white with red crosses that were respected by the Japanese, who flew close enough to be seen waving. It sailed on 12 February after the Japanese signalled they would attack if it remained, and arrived in Batavia on 15 February. The nurses evacuated their wounded and then helped set up a hospital in a con-

Southern Malaya, 16 January 1942. From Allan S. Walker, *Middle East and Far East*, Vol. 2, Series 5 (Medical), *Australia in the War of 1939–1945* (Canberra: Australian War Memorial, 1953).

vent in Batavia until 18 February when they went to Bandung, in the hills inland from Batavia, to the Australian 2/2nd CCS. The precarious military position necessitated their returning to Batavia and on 21 February 1942 they all sailed for Australia in the troopship *Orcades*.

Bennett approved the first evacuation of nurses on the afternoon of 10 February, and indicated the remaining nurses were to embark as soon as practicable. On 11 February the nurses were asked to volunteer to leave; however, as nobody did, evacuation lists were drawn up. Reluctantly, fifty-three nurses from the 2/10th AGH and the 2/13th AGH and seven female masseurs boarded a cargo ship, the *Empire Star*. Betty Jeffrey wrote in her diary, "By Wednesday things were getting very warm and while we were having breakfast at 6.45 a.m. Matron was informed that our hospital [Oldham Hall, 2/10 AGH] was surrounded and we looked like being taken prisoner. There was no panic . . . About 10 a.m. word came for about thirty sisters to go at once . . . off they went hardly anyone to see them go . . ."[6] Each nurse was issued with iron rations, one tin of bully beef or baked beans, a small kitbag and a small haversack; on the wharf some nurses were given tins of baby rusks. The *Empire Star*, a cargo ship, had accommodation for 16 people, but on this voyage it carried servicemen (mostly Royal Air Force), British, Australian and Indian nurses and some civilians — 2154 people in all. The ship departed on the morning of 12 February with Australian nurses accommodated in the meat-hold (the hatch was the only ventilation) when they were not on deck nursing the wounded. The ship was repeatedly dive-bombed, torpedo-bombed and machine-gunned, and received three direct hits. Staff Nurses Margaret I. Anderson and Veronica A. Torney were caught on deck during a raid. They continued to nurse and lay across their patients to protect them when planes dived and machine-gunned the decks. Anderson received the George Medal and Torney an MBE for their bravery. The ship was repaired in Batavia and returned to Australia with the nurses and masseurs.

The remaining sixty-five nurses of the two Australian General Hospitals and 2/4th CCS continued to work until they were ordered to leave on the afternoon of 12 February 1942. Jeffrey wrote in her diary of their distress in leaving: ". . . we just had to walk out on those super fellows lying there — not one complaining and all needed attention — also our young doctors and the senior doctors too — just had to walk out on them — the rottenest thing I've ever done in my life . . . we all hated it — we just sat in that car dazed, it happened so quickly". Jessie Simons recalled argument and indignation were so prevalent that sleeping nightstaff were almost forgotten. There was only time to put a few belongings in a handcase, stuff iron rations into a gas mask and race for waiting ambulances. All the nurses met at St Andrew's Cathedral where some of the troops brought messages to be delivered in Australia and the nurses made their final farewells. The wharf area was so congested the nurses had to walk the final part of the journey through fire, smoke, constant noise and gunfire and "indescribable ruin". They were loaded onto the *Vyner Brooke*, normally equipped to carry twelve passengers but on this, its last voyage, carrying over three hundred, mostly civilian women and children.

Mixed feelings prevailed amongst the nurses; some thought their situation was hopeless, while others anticipated a safe return to Australia. There was one story that they were going to Java to set up hospital till the Japanese were ousted from Malaya and then they would return. The ship slipped out of Singapore harbour that evening, after the final air-raid, to the Australian nurses singing "Waltzing Matilda".

In Rabaul the six nurses had already been captured by the Japanese. They heard radio reports of the attacks on Pearl Harbour, Malaya, Singapore and Hong Kong but it was not until 4 January 1942 that the first bombs were dropped over Rabaul. The nurses were not offered protection and were captured by the Japanese later that month. In December 1941 the Australian War Cabinet had decided to accept the advice of the Australian Chiefs of Staff to leave the garrison at Rabaul by itself, neither extending the forces nor withdrawing them. It was not a vital link in defences or communications and was unable to impose more than an insignificant delay to the enemy.

The War Cabinet had considered voluntary evacuation of the populace from New Britain as early as 17 November 1941. In mid-December compulsory evacuation orders for all European women and children were promulgated, but civilian nurses and missionaries were allowed to remain. The six administration nurses at the European Hospital, one administration nurse at Kavieng and four Methodist missionary nurses volunteered to stay. The civilians left on the *Neptune* and the *Macdhui* on 22 December 1941 and additional evacuees flew out in civil DC3s on 28 December, leaving Rabaul a garrison town.

The nurses in Rabaul were told the Japanese could not fly and that Germans flew their planes! On the afternoon of 20 January 1942 over one hundred Japanese aircraft attacked Rabaul. The Australians suffered devastating defeats, and the nurses worked constantly. On 21 January the remainder of the small airforce was ordered to withdraw to the mainland of New Guinea, leaving 2/22nd Battalion, two coast guns, two anti-aircraft guns and other detachments, all under the command of Colonel J.J. Scanlan, to the Japanese air and naval attacks. There was no order to evacuate the Army nurses with the Royal Australian Air Force or with the last aircraft sent out with wounded on 22 January 1942. They were certain to be caught by the Japanese, but three of the four surviving nurses later emphasized that they felt no bitterness; they still maintain it was their job to stay with the wounded.

Rabaul was evacuated on 22 January 1942, forcing the Army hospital to move to the native hospital at the Roman Catholic mission at Vunapope. During a tropical downpour and constant bombing they transferred the ninety patients and as much equipment as they could fit into trucks; walking patients were sent back to their units. The staff at the European hospital and the four Methodist missionary nurses were also transferred to the mission. There was no time nor room for the Army nurses to collect their clothes or belongings and later their residence was destroyed by a bomb.

The doctors, Major Palmer and Captain Robertson, announced once the hospital had moved that it was "every man for himself", took the two ambulances, most of the medical supplies and the orderlies and left Parker in charge of the newly established hospital. Palmer and Robertson gave valuable medical assistance to the troops still on the island and Palmer eventually escaped. An Anglican chaplain, J. May, assumed responsibility for the hospital and, with two of the orderlies who remained, helped and protected the nurses. With their limited supplies the nurses could do very little. At the time, they were dumbfounded and shocked at their abandonment by the doctors, and the bitterness at being left in such a hopeless situation has not been erased by subsequent knowledge of the doctors' activities in the field.

Sister Parker and Chaplain May surrendered on behalf of the hospital when the Japanese arrived there after landing early on 23 January 1942. Parker handed over a small pistol she carried in her handbag when May decided to lock up the rifles. The nurses expected to be shot or badly treated despite their Red Cross armbands. They were lined up with machine-guns trained on them for a lengthy period in the sun, hoping it would be a quick death, but they were finally released. The Japanese inspected the Army hospital and about every fifth man was taken outside and not seen again. It is believed they were killed and buried in the mass grave found at Kokopo in 1950. The Army and

Methodist nurses were housed in the Dutch convent precinct of the mission; this was their prison until July 1942 when they were moved to Japan. At the convent they were joined by Mrs K. Bignell, a civilian, on 22 February 1942, by the administrative nurses on 25 February, and on 13 March by Sister D.M. Maye, the only administrative nurse at Kavieng, who had been isolated after her capture on 21 January. They lived under constant uncertainty as the Japanese appeared unsure what to do with them.

In less than a year the Australian Army nurses posted to Malaya and Rabaul went from an atmosphere of security and social enjoyment to a hectic period of nursing which lasted barely two months. For thirty-eight of these women the war service which they had hoped to give when they enlisted was denied by years of imprisonment in the hands of captors whose logic they considered unfathomable. The Japanese were unpredictable, sometimes kind and sometimes cruel. They were exposed to unnecessary dangers because conventional military policy, namely that nurses were not to be posted to areas where there was a known risk of being taken prisoner, was ignored. Physically and psychologically unprepared to protect themselves from their captors, they found that the discipline of their profession and the cohesion established before active service were invaluable during the following years of deprivation.

Capture

The *Vyner Brooke*, which had left Singapore on 12 February 1942, was sunk two days later. Thirty-two of the sixty-five Australian Army nurses on board survived, but their Red Cross armbands were ignored and they became prisoners of the Japanese, along with hundreds of civilians. During the initial months they anxiously adjusted to captivity; civilian internment, filth, poor food and harassment by their captors were now the conditions under which they had to live. Compared with the civilians their grouping by virtue of their military identity enabled them to adjust more rapidly to the change.

The *Vyner Brooke* had evaded enemy action during Friday 13 February 1942 as it slowly steamed towards Java. For the nurses it was their first real break for more than a week, although Matron Paschke organized them in distributing amongst the passengers and crew the little food on board (mainly the nurses' bully beef and biscuits as well as a few tins of fruit brought on board by other passengers). Each nurse was allotted an area of the ship and given a task in case of attack; extra field dressings were made and dressings, morphia and syringes pinned inside each nurse's pocket. Matron Paschke also instructed in lifeboat drill and saw that everyone had a lifebelt and knew how to use it.

The foresight of these precautions was evident when the ship was disastrously bombed and strafed on the afternoon of 14 February 1942. Less than thirty minutes later the burning ship sank, but not before the nurses had seen that every civilian was off the ship. There were insufficient lifeboats, and even fewer after the Japanese machine-gunned the deck, but Matron Drummond and some of the nurses, with all the first aid equipment, the wounded, the aged and those who could not swim were loaded into the remainder. The others on board slid down ropes or jumped into the sea and swam amongst Japanese bullets away from the suction created by the sinking ship.

The initial pleasure of the sea after the cramped conditions without water on board was very soon lost as the unpredictable currents of the Banka Strait carried most of the groups throughout the night before they could swim ashore. The life jackets enabled the survivors to grab hold of debris which gave them psychological support and conserved the resources of even those who were strong swimmers. Most of the nurses formed groups with other nurses or civilians. Jessie Simons said, "If I had been alone that night, Davey Jones would have had another visitor to supper. I was numb, cold, stiff and exhausted and my skinned hands were worn raw by the wet, coarse ropes." One group of five staff nurses, Jessie J. Blanch, Jean K. Greer, Florence E. Trotter, Joyce Tweddell and Beryl Woodbridge, with a civilian woman, clung to a ship's rail and set off with Greer singing "We're off to see the Wizard". They hoped the sharks had been well fed!

After sixteen hours of struggling to reach shore they landed on Banka Island, weak, fatigued and chafed by their life jackets. Some had shrapnel wounds. A native gave them coconut milk and directed them to a village, where they were lined up by a Japanese soldier to be shot. Instead they were taken to the Muntok Customs House for the night and then to the primitive Muntok Cinema where there were other prisoners. Florence Trotter (now Mrs Syer) recalled, "We were foolish enough to imagine a nice soft bed and a cup of coffee!" At the cinema a machine-gun was trained on them and conditions were crowded and filthy. Jessie Blanch said, "We were thirsty, hungry, tired, low in spirits and humiliated. About 7.00 that night [15 February 1942] they came with a bucket of water with rum and sugar mixed in it, and a bucket of rice and the news that Singapore had fallen. You can imagine how we felt."[7]

Other groups got to shore on rafts and were similarly menaced by the Japanese. Staff Nurses Jessie E. Simons, Janet P. Gunther (who could not swim) and Sister Winnie M. Davis were on a raft with civilians and sailors, one of whom was so badly burnt Simons wrapped her uniform around him and Davis gave him morphia, but he slipped off the raft during the night. The previous group had been ignored while the Japanese landed on the island, but after Simons gesticulated for assistance a boat collected the women (the men preferred to be towed) and brought them to shore where their fate was disputed. "Our own reactions may be imagined. Tired and weak, we still had a lively interest in the outcome of the discussion, and with heavily beating pulse we tried to follow it and anticipate the result."[8] They were housed in a pigsty that night with the pigs and later taken to the Muntok Cinema. Another group including Staff Nurse Veronica A. Clancy and Sylvia J.M. Muir reached shore on a raft using their uniforms as sails. They landed like Simons in their slips and underwear and were given clothes by the male survivors. Simons recalled:

> One of the guards walked over and pulled out my slip. He looked down my neck, perhaps to decide if I was male or female [Simons had very short hair]. Then he laughed raucously. I remembered vividly the English officer who wanted us shot and just then it did not seem as funny as in Singapore. I drew myself up to my full five feet eight inches and tried to convey a firm but not aggressive reproof. A very delicate situation![9]

Gunther slept the night in the pigsty with an iron bar beside her!

Some of the villagers who lived on Banka Island offered assistance to the nurses. Sister Ellen M. Hannah, who could not swim, was separated from others on her raft when those on board decided to leave and swim in with the tide, but she was rescued by a Malay fisherman who took her ashore by allowing her to hold onto his canoe. He came back in the evening with tapioca root and cold coffee but was too frightened to do anything more for her and those who had congregated with her. Eventually the party decided to give themselves up and were taken to the cinema. Staff Nurses Iole Harper and Betty Jeffrey were in the water for seventy-two hours (the longest of all the nurses), but were eventually collected by a Malay fisherman in a small boat who took them to his village where they were fed and had their injured hands and legs bandaged. The villagers offered to care for them, but a Chinese man who had escaped from the Japanese suggested otherwise. The Japanese put on a show of strength when they collected the women, but as soon as they left the village they were friendly to their two captives. Neither of the two nurses knew each other before their ordeal but from then on they were close friends.

Other women spent most of the time in the water alone. Sister Nesta G. James met a civilian woman just before she reached shore after twelve hours in the water. They were rushed by Japanese with bayonets who took their money and also James's paybook. Staff Nurse Cecilia M. Delforce heard light gunfire and thought it might have been the nurses in trouble but instead discovered a Japanese soldier shooting a line of British and Dutch men. She stood at the end of the line, convinced of the truth of the stories that the Japanese did not take prisoners. Nonplussed the soldier stopped, led her to the nurses inside and did not resume his job. Their policy of not shooting women however was not consistent.

The nurses discovered that Red Cross armbands and protected status had no effect on Japanese treatment. Twenty-two nurses in uniform and wearing armbands were shot on Banka Island by Japanese soldiers. These nurses (some of them injured) had landed in lifeboats during the night of 14 February and lit a huge bonfire for the others to reach. Most of the other nurses tried to get to the bonfire and civilian men, women and children as well as English servicemen did join them.

After investigating the surroundings they decided to surrender as there was no possible escape and no food, and they reasoned that the Japanese would not kill one hundred unarmed people. A small party of men went looking for the Japanese, and Matron Drummond suggested the civilian women follow with the restless children. The nurses remained with the injured, made stretchers for those who could not walk and erected a large red cross to show they were non-combatants. One civilian woman also remained to care for her injured husband. A group of about twenty Japanese soldiers arrived from Muntok and, ignoring their explanations, took the fifty or so men down the beach behind a bluff. The women heard muffled gunfire, and the Japanese returned wiping their bayonets. The twenty-three women were then ordered into the sea. "The conduct of all the girls was most courageous. They all knew what was going to happen to them but no one panicked: they just marched ahead with their chins up."[10] Staff Nurse Vivian Bullwinkel, the sole survivor, recalled one girl saying, "Two things I hate in life — Japs and water — and I've got them both." Bullwinkel continued:

> I was near the end of the line on the right. We waded into the surf and were almost up to our waists in the water when they just fired on us from behind. I don't think anybody screamed. We weren't even frightened. There was no panic, no hysteria, no tears. We just accepted it as being our lot.

Bullwinkel was hit in the left loin and knocked into the sea, where she remained conscious but feigned death. She drifted in and crawled into the jungle where she watched a line of armed soldiers go back to the

34

beach and then leave. Later an Englishman, Private Kingsley, who had received a bayonet wound whilst on his stretcher and was left for dead, called out to her. She found none of the nurses. The two of them lived in the jungle for twelve days on water from freshwater springs, and rice, fish and pineapple which the local village women gave them despite the hostility of the male villagers. When Kingsley felt stronger, they decided it was better to be shot than die of starvation. They waited until Kingsley had his thirty-ninth birth-day and then gave themselves up. Kingsley died a few days later.

They were caught on the way to Muntok on 28 February but, as agreed, neither mentioned the massacre when questioned, and Bullwinkel held a water bottle over the bullet mark in her bloodstained dress. She was taken to a large barracks where the other nurses were collected, but broke down after the nurses persistently asked whether she had seen any of the girls that she knew had been shot. The nurses were advised by Australian Intelligence officers, whom they called Mr Wooten and Mr Quinn, and who had also been captured, that they were not to mention the ex-perience again as they would all be at risk. For the duration of the war the subject was strictly forbidden. Bullwinkel was protected by the other nurses, in-dicative of the security the group provided. A reserved woman with a keen sense of humour, Bullwinkel main-tained that her attitude to captivity was consequently different from that of the other women. She said:

> I went into prison camp in a very different frame of mind pro-bably to the other girls because when I was out in the jungle I

said all I want is to get back amongst my own people, I don't care how long I'm taken prisoner. So that when we began to feel a bit frustrated or feel when is this going to end, I'd remind myself of what I said . . .

Sister Carrie J. Ashton, Senior Sister of the 2/13th AGH members in camp, agreed Bullwinkel had "more courage to carry on regardless".

The other twelve nurses missing from the *Vyner Brooke* are believed to have been killed by falling debris, drowned, or died from wounds, lack of water and starvation.

The male service personnel tried to impress upon the Japanese that the nurses were military personnel and non-combatants, but their arguments were useless. For example, in July 1942, the officers in Changi heard of the fate of the nurses on the *Vyner Brooke* and Major-General C.A. Callaghan, GOC, made several appeals to the Japanese through Headquarters Malaya Command that they be repatriated, or at least transferred to the care of the AIF in Singapore. Although some diplomatic and civilian personnel were exchanged in the Far East when food and medicine were despatched, representations by the British Commonwealth and Allied nations and the Protecting Power, Switzerland, to repatriate POWs held by Japan were denied, despite German and Italian acceptance of repatriation.

The Japanese tradition of bushido demanded that Japanese should fight until death; surrender was shameful. Colonel Tokunago Isao, the overall commander of all prison camps in Hong Kong, maintained in 1946 that POWs were disgraced by surrender and even Japanese women and children would die rather than become POWs. Despite the fact that two Japanese nurses visited the women's camp in Sumatra in 1944 and injections were given to the women infrequently throughout captivity, the Japanese did not have an organized medical system like that of their enemy. They did not have the same respect for life towards their own forces, let alone internees. As women, the internees — and the Army nurses were classified as internees — were treated with indifference or as sexual objects and workers.

Although Japan had ratified the Red Cross Convention it had no legal obligation to provide humane treatment as it had not ratified the Convention on Treatment of Prisoners of War (27 July 1929, Geneva). This enumerated standards of care for those who were captured and included dietary, disciplinary and environmental requirements. The Prime Minister of Japan, Tojo, who also held the positions of Minister for Home Affairs and Minister for War, and thus had control over Police as well as Army, agreed to apply the Convention on Treatment of Prisoners of War and take into consideration the national standards of American, Australian, British, Canadian and New Zealand POWs and internees in January, February and March 1942. Postwar investigations, however, established that as early as the end of 1942 Tojo issued a directive to all camp commandants that prison rations were to be cut in order to conserve food for Japanese workers and armed forces; a year later a dictum "no work no food" was issued, which may account for the treatment of the female prisoners, particularly in Sumatra. Moreover, the Eastern diet, confined living space and communal ablutions, to which Europeans found difficulty adjusting, did not appear to perturb the Japanese who lived under similar conditions.

The twenty-nine nurses in the filthy Customs House and cinema carried the wounded men on improvised stretchers to the Chinese "coolie" barracks where the soldiers, sailors, airmen and women were housed for two weeks. Jeffrey, Harper and later Bullwinkel joined them there. The nurses were suffering from shock, exposure, lacerated feet (as most had kicked off their shoes when they jumped), chafe from their life jackets, and swollen legs as well as various wounds from shrapnel and falling wreck debris. Many of the nurses also developed diarrhoea which they attributed to their new rice diet; for some this was a continuous problem for the next three years. Vivian Bullwinkel's wound healed despite lack of immediate medical care. Jessie Simons recalled: "Iole Harper and Betty Jeffrey came in . . . Physically they were wrecks, but still cheerful." They were covered with infected mosquito and sandfly bites. Rope burns due to the hasty escape from the ship immobilized the hands of some including Jeffrey and Simons, so the other nurses washed and fed them. It was from these early times that mutual support groups amongst the nurses originated and grew stronger.

During this period the Japanese ignored them except to rap the feet of the prisoners with torches, hit their legs with their bayonets or flash light in their faces when they were sleeping. With the civilian nurses, who had also formerly been in Malaya and had also been shipwrecked, the Army nurses staffed a dormitory that was used as a hospital. Three female doctors, two British and one German, and the nurses tended the sick and wounded with the pooled medical supplies, one towel and no soap. Nesta James and another nurse were also taken to the local airfield to tend the POWs, civilians and "coolie" labour working there. The nurses who could not work played bridge, talked and wandered around the compound.

The unhygienic conditions and lack of privacy appalled the nurses, accustomed as they had been to hospital cleanliness and order. About six hundred people, survivors of numerous shipwrecks, inhabited concrete barracks that were built in a U-shape. The roof material was tin and the inmates slept on bare concrete floors. The men and women each had one arm of the building, the Japanese the connecting link, and the surrounding area was used as an exercise yard. Forty cramped inmates lay twenty abreast each side of the dormitory, invariably slipping down a level during the night on the sloping floor. One nurse exclaimed, "The air was putrid." At the bottom of the dormitory ran unprotected concrete drains which served as lavatories for the Japanese and prisoners.

It was shocking. We were very crowded and had nothing but cement to lie on and no clothes or cover, no mosquito nets all night. The Japanese would walk to and from the women's barracks and hit us. They were to and fro all the time with their bayonets. They came into the lavatories, which had no doors; it was just a cement latrine and they made themselves objectionable to us in the lavatories, also in the place where we managed to bath.[11]

The reaction of some of the girls was not to use the lavatory at all. Bath water trickled from a large trough-like concrete bath called a *tong*; the prisoners had to stand outside and throw water over their bodies. Simons said, "Crude and filthy native latrines were the only provisions and we had to become used to Japanese guards wandering indifferently through them and around the *tongs*." The water was very dirty and not improved by the "indiscriminate habits of some of the internees who washed their filthy clothes in the communal bath".

Water and food were strictly rationed with drinking water limited to a mugful per person per day. Meagre rations of burnt rice and foul-tasting tea were issued in the morning and at 4.00 p.m. they were given more grey rice and stew occasionally supplemented by food they scrounged. Jeffrey described the meal as "a piece of vegetable, possibly potato, the size of a threepence, or perhaps a tiny splinter, one to each bowl, which we were told was pork. Sometimes we had what was called coffee . . . a faint resemblance of the real thing". Some of the men volunteered to stand in the food lines for the nurses, which some of the civilian women resented. Simons commented, ". . . our first experience of fierce elemental selfishness which throughout our captivity we found mixed with sublime endurance and self sacrifice. The polite veneer of civilization had begun to crack". Unwilling to eat with their fingers, the nurses collected chipped rice bowls, broken spoons, chopsticks, bent butter knives and a shoe horn left behind by former inmates, which became their cutlery and crockery in the following years. By the end of the war spoons were worn down by constant scratching for the last bit of food. They also cut down the trousers of the Allied sailors who had been the previous inmates of the barracks, into shorts and tops as their own uniforms were covered in oil and dirt. Civilians gave them clothes and the Japanese allowed Simons's group to search a deserted house where they collected blouses and sarongs that formed the bases of their wardrobe. Everything had a purpose, even cloth fragments were used to protect them from the mosquitoes.

The routine established at the barracks was shattered a few days after Bullwinkel's arrival when they were moved in unprotected boats and trucks through streets of jeering natives to Palembang, Sumatra. The civilian men, women and children were settled in former Dutch bungalows in Bukit Besar (Big Hill), a suburb of Palembang. The nurses still considered themselves military personnel and moved into two houses separated from the rest of the camp by another two houses whose Dutch inhabitants had not been evicted. The 2/13 AGH and the 2/4th CCS had one house and the 2/10th AGH the other. The rest of the internees endeavoured to find compatible people to share the houses designed for six people that now had about seventeen people in each. Families and service officers' wives gathered together and national and socio-economic distinctions were recognized. The Dutch who had not been interned, and Malay women who had worked for the dispossessed Dutch, brought them extra food, toothbrushes, clothes, cushions and games. Rations improved for the first two weeks and were mostly a type of spinach and their own army biscuits. The bits of furniture, normal cooking facilities and the prospect of a little more privacy raised the nurses' spirits considerably. Simons remarked, "We were together again under conditions that reminded us remotely of our bungalows at Singapore."

The Japanese wandered in and out of the showers inspecting any females but it was not until the nurses were evicted from their houses, which became the Japanese Club, that there was any suggestion of their becoming Japanese "girlfriends". When the nurses moved into the neighbouring empty Dutch homes, they took everything including flyscreens and light fittings. "On Sunday afternoon in the pouring rain we moved next door, furniture, stove and all over the fence — team work excellent — one person every few yards as the couch, armchairs etc. passed down the file and over the fence."[12] The following week six nurses were ordered to scrub out three houses on the other side of the suburb which they euphemistically called "Lavender Street" after a red light district in Singapore. An English woman married to a Singapore Chinese, Mrs Chan, tried to recruit females to work in the club, but the response was so poor the Australian nurses were ordered to attend opening night. That day some of the nurses were asked to sign an "I am willing to entertain the Japanese officers" form which they refused to do, thus evoking the Japanese response that they would die!

Rather than choose eight women to attend the opening night they all went, except for a few who were sick.

Hannah rationalized that as she was too weak to fight "what is to be, will be" but it would never hurt the real her. One nurse decided she would choose one man, preferably the doctor, and concentrate her efforts on him rather than be the "plaything" of all of them. Another suggested they should teach them to play cards and someone else advocated that they should all promise never to mention the incident. They arrived at the club looking as ugly and filthy as they could in their dirty uniforms, bare feet or oversized shoes, and unruly hairstyles. Two Englishmen volunteered to act as barmen, one in each house, and their presence at least raised morale. The nurses' unexpectedly large numbers — in one house fourteen nurses met only two Japanese officers — were to their advantage. They were given peanuts and biscuits (stealing as much as they could), drank soft drinks as agreed instead of proferred liquor and refused the opportunity to buy lipstick and powder in town. The fourteen nurses were finally sent away but the other nurses were forced to leave four of their number behind after the civilian camp commandant, Mr Miachi, called them aside and told them if they did not acquiesce they would be starved — the Army was totally in control of the food supply on the island. Four of the nurses volunteered to stay. Staff Nurse Pauline B. Hempsted, an imposing woman, feigned a tubercular cough which sent the officer running immediately. Hannah, who was taller than her "suitor", pushed him over when he told her he "loved" her and he let her go home, and Valerie Smith and Staff Nurse Eileen M. Short, both strong women, kept their "suitors" walking until they were tired and let them return to their friends.

The following day another four nurses, including Nesta James and Staff Nurse Jess G. Doyle, attended a board of three officers who informed them that they had to "work" for the Japanese or starve. They refused and during the following week rations were cut and they were reduced to eating tapioca root which grew in one of the yards. Jeffrey wrote in her diary, "I really think the mental strain was far worse than even being shipwrecked, bombed and sunk." Simons recalled, "For two weeks after this we were under enormous tension, and became mentally worn with expectation. Any sound, at night especially, set our hearts beating." One of the camp medical officers, a Scotswoman Dr J. McDowell, got word to a former Red Cross representative who informed the Japanese Resident in Palembang and soon after the club closed. Whatever the reason for the closure, other women in the camp were willing to trade sex for favours. Iole Harper said, "There were plenty there who were quite happy to have it on so why bother about haggish looking nurses? You've got 500 or something women, and at least fifty of those who are only too anxious. They'd be given food and money, and if that was their scene, why not?"[13]

This experience made the nurses wary of Japanese suggestions and from then on they insisted nursing was the only work they were willing or capable of doing. Some of the internees earned money by sewing Japanese loincloths, but the nurses reasoned that their strength lay in unobtrusive non-cooperation. In September Mr "Ask-what-you-like-you-won't-get-it" Miachi called for volunteers from the Australian, British, Chinese and Dutch nurses to nurse Allied white men working in the Pladjoe oilfields near Palembang. All the nurses met to discuss the proposal but only about twenty half-heartedly volunteered on the basis that Allied men had asked for them. The Australians refused; Nesta James suggested that there be a full investigation but this never eventuated. In a statement after the war James said she had met Dutchmen who worked in those oilfields who denied asking for sisters to nurse them. Some weeks later Miachi requested volunteers to nurse Japanese soldiers in hospital, but only a few agreed and again not the Australians. The scheme was not implemented but three houses at their new residence were taken away as punishment.

The Australians' caution proved to be well founded. Four British nurses (two civilians and two members of the Queen Alexandra's Imperial Military Nursing Service) were taken to work at a native hospital, run by a Dutch and an Indonesian doctor, after the camp move to Irenelaan in April 1942. They worked there until April 1943 when they were put in jail for no apparent reason. Two nurses were put in each cell. The cells were large enough for the nurses to walk four paces — that was their exercise. For the next six months they lived in appalling conditions, with nothing to do. In July the four nurses were put in one cell and witnessed many of the other inmates in the jail being tortured and beaten. Unexpectedly in September 1943 they were returned to the women's camp.

In March the rumours of exchange began and persisted throughout the war, but the only movement was to Irenelaan, the Women's Internment Camp Palembang, on April Fool's Day 1942. Four hundred women and children had to live in fourteen three-roomed houses and garages in Irenelaan so the loss was felt. Families were unexpectedly separated when the men were taken to the Palembang jail and the women and children marched to Irenelaan on the other side of Palembang. They carried everything movable but the guards searched for knives and other possible weapons which the nurses hid for non-aggressive purposes. As they left their bungalows at Bukit Besar a guard whistled "Home, Sweet Home".

The first two months of captivity were ones of rapid adjustment from positions of respect and importance to the status of mere civilian internees. Survival skills were acquired and the nurses' characteristic caring and solidarity emerged in this early period when the multifarious group of people had to become accustomed to camp life. Staff Nurse Blanch (now Mrs Jessie Eaton-Lee) wrote:

> We did have our bad times, that dreadful feeling in the tummy — just didn't know what the Japs would do as we were at their mercy. I think now that feeling was with me most of the time — that was why it was so important to have interests, which we did try to have. We are a very close group — a wonderful and understanding bond.

After the initial months of uncertainty they developed a routine of camp organization and communal activities. Suspicion and fear of the Japanese did not daunt their spirit.

Irenelaan — A New Home

For the next eighteen months, four hundred Australian, British, Eurasian, Dutch and various other nationalities were accommodated at Irenelaan where they established an ordered existence. Each house developed a daily plan and on the camp level the residents elected spokeswomen and committees to organize every aspect of camp life. A number of the Australian and British inhabitants, the poorer members of the camp, developed ingenuity and creativity in coping with internment. These activities added interest to their otherwise monotonous lives and raised morale.

Formerly a Dutch residential suburb, the Irenelaan camp consisted of small, relatively new bungalows intended to house three to four people, in two adjoining tree-lined streets, which made an attractive setting but were inadequate for the number of internees. The Dutch, when they were finally interned, arrived in comparative affluence, having observed the Japanese treatment of the predominantly British internees. They had money and valuables, pots and pans, bedding, sewing machines, a typewriter, and proper clothes and footwear, which made the basic surroundings more comfortable. Bungalows, some with two bedrooms, a lounge-dining room, a bathroom and a kitchen outside, housed up to thirty-six internees; garages took fifteen. The 2/10 AGH nurses and seven other women lived in one bungalow and the 2/13th AGH and the 2/4th CCS nurses lived next door in another bungalow, with five other women and three children. Most of the houses had been stripped of furniture and the water and electricity had been disconnected (although they were eventually turned on). There were no stoves, fuel, cooking pots, or food when they first arrived, so the Australians acquired water, smashed down the door for firewood and cooked rice in a Mobil oil tin which, though cleared of oil and spider webs, flavoured the rice and tea for weeks. The meal provided was greatly appreciated by the other internees, some of whom had been invalids before the war. They slept on cold tiles in the houses or on dirty cement floors in the garages, with tiny cushions or lifebelts or pieces of wood or books as pillows.

Diminutive Nesta James slept in a cot, though this was eventually reduced to one small side-piece, to keep her off the tiles, when the wood crisis necessitated that everything, including wardrobes and beams, be used for firewood. Open drains, running alongside the house then into the street, and septic tanks overflowed as neither could cope with the needs of more than three to four people. In some of the garages the only lavatory was a hole in the ground outside. James said, "The sanitation was ghastly . . . No rubbish of any kind was collected from that camp. The rubbish was just left lying there." They were told they were staying overnight in this camp, but instead barbed wire entanglements and a guardhouse were organized. James commented, "At this camp we felt safer, no one was allowed into the camp except the Japanese guards who were looking after us." They were protected from some of the natives who they felt might have loose morals and were insulated within their own society.

The rations were generally adequate in quantity but very monotonous and unsustaining to the Western palate. Jeffrey wrote, "We could smell decayed vegetables and bad Chinese cabbages long before the truck bringing them arrived in camp." Occasionally a wild pig called a "moving mass" would be thrown onto the roadway and surrounded by dogs which the internees were not allowed to chase away. A Japanese guard placed his boot on the meat to steady it and cut pieces the size of a small palm of a hand for each house. A small number of cucumbers, a vegetable like spinach, *bringals* (like eggplant) and long beans were their staple vegetables for months; when made into a stew each person received a dessertspoonful. They became accustomed to eating all kinds of waterlily roots, bamboo shoots and bad leeks that added flavour to their bland repast. Infrequently they were given a bad egg to be shared among three people. Sometimes they were only issued rice which had to be eaten plain as they were not given salt until May and irregularly thereafter. The nurses vied with each other to disguise the ubiquitous rice. They made rice "cakes", "pastries" and "puddings". The most common method of cooking it was to make a thin porridge, sometimes flavoured with sugar, *gula java* (a sickly sweet) or coconut milk, which was at best hot, wet and filling. On very rare occasions they were supplied with tapioca root; this was ground with rice in a looted coffee grinder, salt and water were added, the dough was steamed and the resulting slab was called bread. "Our morale during this month [June] was no doubt elevated by the diet — for thirty days we had disintegrating cabbage, beans (the long and short with the tall), eggs, duck of course, or yak — with, naturally, rice and the protein therein found in the shape of weevils and worms."[14]

In August 1942 a Chinese trader Gho Leng was allowed into the camp with a bullock cart filled with overripe pineapples, green bananas, coconuts, limes, *gula java*, sugar, herbs, spices, tea and coffee as well as other foods, and footwear (most of the British were barefoot). "Thank heaven our diet improved! We were simply craving for sugar, for we had been given one ration only during this six months, and then only two pounds for the whole house. We were also longing for fruit — the joy of having a whole banana to yourself! Pineapple, too, was wonderful after months of soggy rice."[15] The Dutch could take advantage of this and also use the dangerous black market, but the Australians and most of the British had to devise methods to obtain money.

The nurses and the British reasoned that the only way to get money was to do jobs for, or sell goods to, the Dutch. Soya beans were comparatively plentiful, unappetizing and indigestible but rich in vitamin B. Some of the nurses sold all kinds of soya bean products such as soya milk made from soaking and pounding the beans then adding flavouring, and these were in great demand. Davis, Hannah, Jeffrey and Simons made sweets from *gula java*. Hannah and Simons developed a strong working partnership which lasted throughout captivity. They manufactured straw hats from native grass bags, with cotton and trimmings supplied by the customers who were invariably Eurasian. They sold these for one and a half guilders, quite a lucrative business as their turnover in the first year ran into hundreds. These sources of income did not, however, keep pace with rising prices or the insufficiency of goods. The nurses were reluctant to use the black market as any natives caught were cruelly dealt with; one native was tied at the foot of the 2/10th AGH house with barbed wire and left to die. The Japanese would not allow anyone near him and severely beat one white woman who tried to give him a drink.

The lack of water was a major problem. The hilltop location of the camp reduced the flow of water through the pipe system to a trickle so they had to rise early to get the day's water supply; otherwise they had to carry it up the steep hill later in the heat of the day or go without. A few months after occupation the taps were turned off so they queued at the last house of the camp and got their water requirements from one tap. The first soap ration in May 1942 enabled them to have their first proper wash since Singapore. The lack of soap combined with scarcity of water made personal cleanliness and a hygienic sanitary system very difficult to attain.

The nurses organized themselves into a daily routine, taking turns cooking, housekeeping and district nursing. Every day a squad of three people would cook and wash-up for the house. A resigned Jeffrey wrote, "It is a long day of jolly hard slogging, since the cooks must be up by 6.30 a.m. Once 'cooking day' is over we can relax for a few days before it comes round again. Cooking rice and oddments three times a day for twenty-four people and trying to ring the changes is some contract." In the 2/10th AGH house, two housekeepers "scrubbed" the floors of the house with an old tin helmet (that one of the nurses had worn when she jumped overboard) filled with water and old rags; the other housekeeper cleaned the drain outside with a heavy hoe, washed the porches and collected the rations.

Medical staff were already vitally required. A community nursing committee established a dressing station in one of the garages, which was also the residence of the British camp commandant, Dr McDowell, and other nurses made house calls — "district nursing". The overcrowded and unhygienic camp, combined with the deteriorating health of internees from lack of protein and vitamins, was already giving rise to deficiency diseases. The largely starch diet gave the inmates the appearance of being fat as they had swollen legs and distended "rice bellies". Several of the nurses complained of neuritis of the hands and feet, which they blamed on the concrete floors, although about that time, August 1942, several were admitted to the hospital diagnosed with beri-beri. Dysentery spread during the first six months but malaria was not a problem despite the droves of mosquitoes. The Japanese did not supply medication. Only the very sick were taken to the Dutch Charitas Hospital in Palembang run by Roman Catholic Dutch nuns and three doctors, who also treated civilian men and servicemen from nearby prison camps.

> It is only small and is an awful place. There is no ventilation in the wards at night; everything has to be closed because of mosquitoes and Japanese. I spent a week there after having an appendical attack, then begged to go back to camp in spite of having a wooden bench, a mattress and a pillow to sleep on. We were packed in that ward at night like sardines and we all hated it.[16]

The nuns arranged for some medication to be smuggled into the internment camps although their own supplies were not complete. They had been evicted from their new hospital to this building when the Japanese had seized the former for their own sick and wounded. They were only allowed to take the beds and an operating table but they transferred drugs, medicines and even surgical equipment in their habits, and added them to supplies they had already hidden.

The hospital became a place of intrigue where men and women, admitted on the pretext of some illness, would meet in the unguarded community lavatories, exchange news, food, names and money. The servicemen were given small payments for work they did for the Japanese and gave seventy-five cents a week to each of the destitute persons in the women's camp; this was added to a general camp fund raised by concerts and bazaars. The Japanese soon realized that systems of exchange were in practice, and more devious means had to be designed. Mavis Hannah was one of the carriers, hiding letters and money for the sick in an unused sanitary napkin. On one occasion she made contact with an Englishman who gave them a hundred guilders. She was finally exposed, interrogated and severely beaten by the Japanese secret police, the Kempei Tai. The money bought sandals, some material for necessary clothing and extra food.

There was friction amongst the nationalities of the camp because of different traditions, customs, personalities and jealousies. The 2/10th AGH house acquired a Malay family, "lousy with scabies and fleas", whose hygiene and cooking standards were beneath those required by the nurses. The 2/13th AGH girls in house seven shared with an Irish family who lived in a "filthy, stinking, noisy atmosphere all day long". The two groups rearranged their bedding with the prospect of another family joining them but as this did not eventuate the Irish family demanded a return to the previous situation. Ashton, the house captain, tried to conciliate but the nurses refused to move; the Irish mother retaliated by grabbing one nurse by the hair and one of her daughters, armed with a knife, yelled abuse such as "officers' playthings" and "you ran out on Singapore". Eventually in January 1943 the Australians swapped rooms with the group of civilians in the 2/10th AGH house. The nurses had not lived together previously because they considered a three-roomed bungalow too small for thirty-two people.

The nurses also had to be careful of pro-Japanese factions in the camp. A tall Javanese guard (known as "Fifth Columnist" because he always wore dark glasses) intercepted a note to the Japanese guards asking that the Army nurses be removed to the paddy fields. He gave it to a Dutchwoman, his former employer and a friend of the nurses; she passed it on to the nurses who destroyed it.

Despite these divisions and conflicts between the wealthier Dutch and the generally poor British, community solutions evolved. Many of the British as well as the Dutch had come from socially and financially affluent backgrounds where they had been accustomed to a gracious lifestyle, but they were all forced to live and work under the same hardship.

Problems that affected the whole camp were resolved by community action. The natural leaders were the useful women, such as doctors and nurses who could help save lives and nuns and missionaries who gave spiritual support, not the former bastions of refined society. Each house appointed a house captain to act as spokeswoman to the guards and at official community meetings. Nesta James was the most senior Australian nurse and therefore the nurses' spokeswoman. Sister Jean Ashton was elected house captain of the 2/13th AGH house and Sister Pearl B. Mittelheuser of the 2/10th AGH. Both were efficient and calm enough to cope with the difficulties they encountered — lack of food, poor facilities and Japanese non-cooperation. The captain was also responsible for informing the guard how many were at *tenko*, a counting parade instituted by the Japanese to order the camp as well as to humiliate and punish the internees, particularly the class conscious British and arrogant Dutch. Betty Jeffrey said, "One infuriating habit our 'masters' have is counting, what is called *tenko*. We suddenly have to dump everything on the spot and stand outside on the roadway in the midday sun or rain and wait to be counted." During *tenko*, British, Australian and Dutch groups were distinguished. The British section of the camp also had a very political election in November to vote for an official commandant. Dr McDowell, already camp commandant by consensus, was elected and assisted by Mrs Hinch, an American married to the English principal of an Anglo-Chinese Methodist school in Singapore, later an inmate of Changi. The Dutch appointed as their commandant Reverend Mother Laurentia of a teaching order.

Various committees were appointed — a sanitary squad, an entertainment committee, a nursing committee responsible for district nursing and a rations committee. The rations were poorly organized by the Japanese, who did not stop the fittest and strongest seizing the food regardless of others. Purportedly on the grounds that the women wanted to save the Japanese trouble, the unpopular and difficult task of rationing was handed over to the committee. Extras and delicacies were always in short supply — one egg between five was difficult enough but if it was bad, as the eggs frequently were, the dissatisfaction was hard to control.

Jeffrey was appointed to the canteen committee with three British and four Dutch; this was designed to ensure equal distribution of Gho Leng's goods. The guards or the male natives watched while the women did their chores. "At last I have decided on my occupation when I get home — I'm going to be a wharfie and move cargo. I now spend the best part of the hottest mornings in the sun on Sunday, Monday, Tuesday and sometimes Wednesday . . ." The committee also policed the sales of Milwani, an Indian, who sold materials and shoes at exorbitant prices.

The nurses were always short of clothes. Staff Nurse Christian Oxley made garments from string bought from Milwani which she knitted with bicycle wheel spokes. Staff Nurses Wilhelmina Raymont and Ada Syer, like the other nurses, made clothes from materials they collected; the former made a suntop and skirt from a floral curtain and the latter a blouse and a pair of shorts from blackout material. Even lampshade material was used. Some of the Dutchwomen gave them clothes and lent them sewing machines; in this they were more generous than two of the few civilian Australians who possessed ample clothing but refused to share. Uniforms were kept if possible "for the great day when we get home". They acquired men's shoes, wore donations from other women and bought wooden clogs as most of the nurses had kicked off their shoes before they jumped off the *Vyner Brooke*. The clogs cost 10 cents a pair when the women were first taken prisoner but were 250 cents by the end of three years. Hannah recalled, "Unless we had something on our feet, we would have to visit the filthy latrines barefoot and this was revolting!" They also made *trompers*, pieces of wood with a piece of rubber or cloth nailed across the foot to hold them in position. These few possessions were jealously guarded but thieves, they presumed natives, were a constant worry and even the Japanese tried to take their bed coverings at night — one girl tied her blanket to her foot to prevent such a loss.

These difficulties did not prevent the women endeavouring to make themselves as comfortable and as mentally alert as possible. Rice sacks stuffed with grass were used as beds, as were cupboards and the top of the piano in the 2/13th AGH house. A neighbouring Dutch house captain could find no use for this piano which occupied valuable bed space so the 2/13th nurses in house seven took it and started Saturday night community sing-a-longs. These pioneering efforts developed into full-scale variety evenings with singing, skits and dancing performed by the British and Dutch. Usually the success of the evening was an act by the nurses such as "Ration Parade" or "Paula of Palembang", a skit featuring camp fashions! These concerts became so popular they repeated performances so everyone could enjoy them. Simons wrote, "We acquired quite a reputation, and often had unofficial audiences outside the house. Even the Nips came and enjoyed our efforts, including parodies directed at themselves which fortunately they could not understand." Miss Margaret Dryburgh, an English teaching missionary in her late fifties who had lived in the East for many years, played the piano accompaniment for these evenings, organized a glee club and taught in the camp school. She also helped edit the *Camp Chronicle* (the Irenelaan newspaper with a British and Dutch editorial board), which included articles written by inmates, a popular cookery section, a children's section, a crossword, camp activities and gossip. It was typed on the camp typewriter on the meagre supply of paper that extended to two copies each month (it only lasted a short while), and was passed around the houses; it never kept abreast of the rumours on which the camp thrived. In June the camp looked forward to a repatriation trip to India via Singapore and in November the destination was Lourenço Marques in southeast Africa. Even a verse circulated to that effect:

> There are some young women who hope
> To travel by sea to the Pope
> And there be exchanged
> As the old boy arranged
> And so, back to our homes and some soap.

Rumours occasionally appeared to be substantiated, as in April 1942 when the Indo-Dutch and Dutch-Eurasians were released. Jeffrey said, ". . . we don't know why but good luck to them". Their spirits were further elevated in May 1942 when Mr Miachi asked the camp inmates to fill out detailed questionnaires requiring their name, age, birthplace, mother's and father's names, latest occupation, cash, valuables and property, "wife's nationality and born place", and where they were living. Jeffrey wrote in her diary on 16 October 1942, "As we are still here now we are still wondering?"

Daily distractions were organized to pass the time. Jeffrey wrote that bridge and contract bridge "help to make the week go quickly". The cards were made from discarded photographs of the former Dutch inhabitants, the backs of which were coloured with red and blue pens borrowed from Dutch friends. Some of the nurses manufactured mah-jong sets from broken doors and furniture which they smoothed with sandpaper leaves. Drawing lessons were given by a Dutch nun, French was taught by a French national, Mrs G. Gilmour, and Dutch and Malay were also taught. A library was established with donations from the internees with frivolous matter predominating. English-speaking Dutch translated Dutch books which were in greater supply. General knowledge discussion groups were formed, Staff Nurse Dorothy Gardam gave a talk on Tasmania, Iole Harper one about life on an Australian sheep station, and Eileen Short spoke about a Queensland cattle station. Miss Dryburgh and Mrs Nora Chambers, an Englishwoman married to a government engineer in Malaya, combined their musical skills and formed a choir which sang at church services and secular occasions. Protestant church services were organized by the missionaries in Miss Dryburgh's garage and the Roman Catholics could attend services at the Dutch nuns' quarters. The services were so well attended women sat in the driveway and garden outside.

Significant occasions were still observed. The British and Australians held an impromptu service for Armistice Day 1942 organized by an Englishwoman and Jean Ashton. The nurses wore their ragged uniforms but most were barefoot. Jeffrey related, "This service was a bit harrowing and I think we were all glad when it was over." The following year the Australians held an Anzac Day service that was equally emotional. Birthdays were always celebrated even if the presents were flowers from the Chinese cemetery behind the camp; Jeffrey's birthday cake was a decorated upturned tin. Everyone "knew" each other's families and their birthdays were also celebrated.

Christmas arrived rapidly and unexpectedly. "We were so sure we would be home for Christmas and nobody gave it much of a thought, but December is going by and we are still very much here — O.K., we can take it, but what is next?"[17] The men's and women's camps were allowed to exchange gifts and the Australian nurses put together a mah-jong set and a stuffed kangaroo, made from a shirt, for the Australian servicemen. Presents were made for the children including appliqued cloth books, games and sweets. The British and Dutch men at the jail sent bully beef, coffee, soap and some pineapples and the men's camp sent the women's camp a large piece of beef, some onions and potatoes. The Japanese contribution had come the day before — they sold the internees a duck egg each. Christmas dinner was their first decent meal since captivity. Christmas pudding was made from brown rice, peanuts, beans, cinnamon and *gula java* and they also had coconut ice supplied by a Dutch friend. Oxley and Greer made a small Christmas tree and decorated it, "so things were not so bad at all, even in an internment camp". Similar festivities were organized throughout the camp. The Japanese brought in Christmas greetings from England, America and Australia. The Australian message read: "Australia sends greetings. Keep smiling. Curtin." The nurses were still interned in the New Year. "New Year's Eve was celebrated very differently this year and rather quietly — no question everybody is sober as judges. We were all invited next door to see the rottenest year everyone of us had ever put in, go out, and a decent new one come in. It was going to be a problem trying to

61

keep awake as we usually go to bed at 9 o'clock, but it was easy."[18] The men's camp provided another delicious dinner. "It is a great comfort to know those men are there not so far away." The women cut fifteen-foot charred lengths of wood with two blunt axes for the whole camp until the men's camp convinced the Japanese to allow them to cut the wood, and by doing so opened secret means of communication and food for the less well-fed women.

The Convention on Treatment of Prisoners of War, Title III, Section I, Article VIII, provided that belligerents were bound to notify each other through the information bureaus, within the shortest period, of their captured prisoners, and permit prisoners to correspond with their families as soon as possible. In February 1943 the Australian nurses were inspected by a Japanese officer who obtained a full list of their names to send to Australia. Jeffrey wrote in her diary, "Think of it!!! Prisoners for a year and our families haven't been informed — lousy devils." He inspected their quarters and seemed disgusted with the grass mattresses and torn sarongs they slept on, and shocked to hear they had received no milk, soap in decent quantities, paper, sanitary paper, butter, beds nor mosquito nets, and had to buy what little sugar and fruit they had. He noted these things and promised better treatment. He said Australia knew they were in Sumatra, sent her love and told them to keep smiling. They could receive parcels and would be allowed to send a letter of thirty words home. "This interlude of special attention was rather resented by the other women in the camp — by now it was every man for himself and any special privileges were jealously frowned upon."[19] The nurses were relieved that action was to be taken, but their experience with the twenty or so forms they had filled out prior to this did not augur well. However, of the twenty-four who survived, seventeen of these women had their names broadcast over Japanese Radio in March 1943. The others — Blake, Bullwinkel, Greer, Harper, Jeffrey, Smith and Syer — were confirmed POWs in October, November and December 1943, as were the rest of the group.

The nurses felt that the worry was more difficult for their parents who knew nothing of their whereabouts, whereas the internees at least knew they were alive. On 13 March 1943 they were issued POW postcards. Some of the nurses, like Florence Trotter, wrote their letters to sound as ridiculous as possible so their parents knew it was false.

Staff Nurse F.E. Trotter to Trotter family, 16 March 1943

My Dears . . .

Well here I am again and believe me it's grand to be able to drop you a line. First and foremost — how are you all? . . . I am very well indeed and so are Blanchie and Tweedie who are rooming with me. Mother could you please write to Mrs Blanch, Alstonville, NSW just in case Blanchie's letter goes astray, also Mrs Tweddell, Norman Park . . . I spend most of my time playing bridge and mahjong and also we have given quite a few concerts to entertain the camp, so you can see time passes rather quickly. Joves, I forgot to say that the cards and mahjong sets are made by our own hands — clever aren't we? — Still it keeps us out of mischief. Mother I have lost my glasses so, if possible to send parcels could you include same . . . there is a lot I would like to say but unfortunately space cramps my style . . . look after yourselves and don't worry about me.

. . . Flo

Others asked for belongings to make their life more comfortable.

Sister E.M. Hannah to Hannah family, 16 March 1943

Dear . . .

Here I am well and unharmed, so don't worry, please. There are 32 of us, including, Raymont . . . Ashton . . . Clancy . . . and Bullwinkel . . . Please communicate with their people . . . As long distance breast-stroke does not permit luggage carrying, I now possess no worldly goods except sun suits and very scanty attire. Please communicate with Red Cross and try and send a letter and parcels, and money if Keswick is able to do so. If possible, washing material, sewing cotton, serviceable shoes, or sand shoes, 4½ size, toilet requisites, Vitamin B Tablets, sun glasses, dried fruits, vegetable seeds, especially carrots, parsnips, lettuce, tomatoes, beans, peas, onions, etc. tinned goods, in fact anything edible or plain, useful wearable things, also books to read, sheets, towels etc. A Shakespeare, Eng. History or something of interest which could be read and studied, would be very useful besides novels. Rice is our staple diet, and has its limitations . . . We play Contract Bridge and Mah Jong. Cards and tiles have been made by us. We have a Choral Class, and have given several concerts for the camp . . . keep smiling, please don't worry. I'm O.K. I hope and pray to see you soon.

. . . Mavis Hannah

Simons asked for glasses as she had lost hers in the sea and for vitamin tablets, neither of which were forthcoming. Most of these letters were received in Australia during December 1943, but goods could not be sent.

Despite these gestures conditions did not improve. In April 1943 rice rations diminished to one cigarette tin per person per day. Gho Leng's supplies dwindled and water was sometimes only available at the guardhouse and then only when the guard permitted. The only time they were clean was when it rained. In June the effort of cooking for thirty-two people became too great so they broke down into groups of two or three, each one called a *kongsi*.

Infection and disease spread, including typhoid. Holes were dug in the jungle alongside the camp to empty bedpans in order to prevent further typhoid cases and the nurses did day and night duty. There was no effective method of stopping infection because the houses were so overcrowded. The nurses were constantly vigilant about their own hygiene and cut their hair for ease and cleanliness. Many of the nurses had stopped menstruating after they jumped overboard whilst others managed with cloth fragments until deprivation ended the problem. After three years of captivity the Japanese finally issued cotton wool and voile-like material for this purpose! Leaves provided

Malaysia: Indonesia West

65

the only toilet paper. The few community toothbrushes they had been given wore out, and their teeth were almost too sore to clean; the Japanese dentist's policy was painful removal of troublesome teeth. Jeffrey described their predicament: "We haven't quite lost hope yet but by hokey if I'm still here next April Fool's Day — I won't be worth saving — can't say I am even now — have grown into a snitchy, bad tempered old spinster and look more like a chook or an old fowl every day." They attempted to keep some vestiges of their former life by "dressing for dinner", which meant changing some item of clothing and washing if there was water, and they "ironed" their clothes by sleeping on them. Certain personalities within the camp were always formally referred to, like Mrs Hinch, and age was respected.

The nurses took an active part in camp life, particularly in this initial period when other internees were not as organized. As unmarried energetic young women they were considered to be capable and suited to manual work. They did the mundane and difficult necessary chores such as wood chopping, wood carrying and maintaining order. Amongst the thirty-two there was always someone who could do the job required and tried to do so with a cheerful demeanour. The other internees sometimes took advantage of their willingness and usefulness. Jeffrey wrote in her diary on 12 March 1943, "I've definitely decided to be a drooping lily when I get out of here — a super drooper in fact — it's the only thing that pays — a girl is a fool to be able to do anything . . ." The trials of community living told upon the internees, culminating in bickering and arguments. However, throughout internment Betty Jeffrey made only one, albeit indirect, adverse comment directed towards her colleagues in her diary and that was in January 1943:

> When I get out of here, heaven preserve me from nagging women, what absolute bliss to be able to be alone for a couple of hours; to be able to sit down and not hear "that's my chair" or "can I have that box you are sitting on" or "I want that small table, hurry up" — why can't a girl sit down in peace and build a Mah Jong set . . . however, I'll try again tomorrow — being Tuesday it's my turn for the chair.

This comment was not reproduced in her book, *White Coolies*, some indication of the protective attitude these women still show to each other. Humour and resilience prevailed. There was very little point in being angry — there was no escape.

The positive spirit that motivated these women perplexed the Japanese. Jeffrey wrote, "I'll swear they don't know what to expect next of us, no wonder they wander around the houses all day with fixed bayonets — they can't understand why we sing so much (so we are told) it somewhat rocks them." It was not only the singing, but their laughter which infuriated the Japanese. The women were ordered to sign "no-escape" forms which some of the nurses refused to sign until a message from the men's camp assured them that it meant nothing.

"NO-ESCAPE" FORM

An oath and a true letter

I sign my hand below, in this internment place and swear in the name of God that I will not run away nor plot ways and means to escape.

If I break this oath whatever punishment is meted out to me I will accept.

Date   Month   Year

Women's Internment Camp Palembang

Name and Initials

The Javanese guards who took over from the Japanese on occasions left the women to themselves whilst they slept on guard duty, played with the children or deloused themselves.

The eighteen months at Irenelaan brought no letters, parcels, repatriation or decent food, but the internees kept reasonably well and active. The nurses with their natural cohesion and the discipline of their calling acted in a professional and social capacity. Hannah recollected, "Yesterday had happened, tomorrow may never come, so one lived each day as best one could. The comradeship of our own band of people helped tremendously. Among so many women of all nationalities, colour etc., we were leaders in many ways, disciplined and caring. Without each other life would have been much harder." The significance of these activities was particularly vital in the following years. By the end of their time at Irenelaan their health was beginning to deteriorate. Some of the Australian nurses were already in hospital as patients. During the next phase of their captivity, their declining health, combined with worse surroundings, military rule and manual work, contributed to the deaths that followed. The air-raid practice and permanent blackout in September 1943 were not followed by the hoped-for release.

White Coolies

The move in September 1943, from the relative tranquillity and contentment of Irenelaan to the men's camp in Sumatra, marked the end of a period of comparative health and well-being. The following two years were marked by a slow decline in energy, disease and death. The military took command of the camp in April 1944 and their demands helped drain the final reserves of the women. The nurses' duties were varied and largely ineffectual, but their caring attitude to each other and to others sustained a hope which could not be substantiated, removed as they were from news of outside events. They knew nothing of the Allied victories nor that the war was entering its final phase. Their lives were centred upon staying alive.

Long *attap* huts set in an unhygienic swampy area composed the new camp. Formerly the civilian men's camp, which the men had built, it was left stripped of everything useful, the wells (there was one tap and three unreliable wells for the camp) were filled with rubbish and there was filth everywhere; the departing men had supposed that the Japanese were to be the new inhabitants. The women spent days making the camp habitable, assisted by their scraps of wire, old tins, bricks to build fireplaces, nails and other materials they had collected in Irenelaan and brought despite their hasty departure.

A wooden shelf two feet from the ground and approximately five feet six inches wide was their bed. Jeffrey said, "We are sixty to one hut and lie alongside each other like sardines." In early 1944 the nurses' dormitory was divided in half; eight Indonesians training to be guards were accommodated on one side and twenty-six nurses on the other. Jeffrey wrote, "We have all had to move up and our bed-space is now marked on the wooden ledge. You do *not* go over your line! Twenty and a half inches by five feet six inches and no air — it is terrific!" Some of the nurses could not stand the hot, sticky climate so they slept outside on the crude dinner benches or in the shelter shed, dodging leaks all night. The British nurses were allotted twenty-seven inches: ". . . in this we had to keep all our personal belongings — not that there were many — and some women got annoyed if one was an inch over the allotted space. We were all living in such close proximity and under such trying conditions that I am afraid tempers did fray a bit."[20]

There was no privacy. The camp had two bathrooms, one each for the British and Dutch subjects. The British bathroom had two taps, neither of which worked, so the roof over the *tong* was torn off. The water came through and the sun dried the women; there were few towels. This communal bathing upset the sensibilities of some of the women and even Miss Phyllis Briggs, formerly a civilian nurse, was repulsed by the ugliness of the human form: "The women were either very thin and scraggy or else had swollen rice tummies and legs and most of them had septic sores and mosquito bites."[21] The lavatory was a long cement drain and the septic tank had to be cleaned daily otherwise it overflowed. The women emptied this and the drains as the Japanese would not let the natives do it for them. Vivian Bullwinkel and Staff Nurse Wilma E.F. Oram were part of the British and Dutch cleaning squad.

The years of internment had diminished the health of the internees. The men's camp was thick with bugs, fleas, rats, all kinds of vermin and vicious ants that the natives called "fire ants", but no insecticide was issued despite requests. Malaria outbreaks were common owing to the swampy locality. Dengue fever, dysentery, skin diseases, bronchitis and myocarditis affected some of the nurses. Many people suffered rheumatism which worsened during the wet season as they were ankle-deep in mud. Among the nurses only two with typhoid fever were considered seriously ill. The nurses barrier-nursed these two women. There was no soap and very little water, but hot water was kept aside to help prevent the infection from spreading.

The Australian and British nurses undertook district nursing as only the very sick went into the camp hospital. There were few medical supplies so all they could do was make sure their patients ate, drank and were clean and comfortable. They gave advice and more importantly cared for those who did not have any other support. The Dutch nursing nuns ran the camp hospital within the camp. The doctor-in-charge, Dr

Goldberg, a German Jewess, was very thorough but occasionally she was anti-Australian and would refuse to admit Australian nurses, although on another occasion she raised forty guilders to provide tinned milk for their two typhoid victims. The Japanese contribution to medical care was negligible but the internees were innoculated to prevent disease:

1943	March	Dysenteric vaccine
	April	TAB Vaccine
	July	TAB (2 injections)
		Cholera
		Dysenteric vaccine
1944	August	Dysenteric vaccine (2)
		TAB (2 injections)
		Cholera (2 injections)
1945	May	Smallpox vaccination
	August	Dysenteric vaccination
		Cholera
		TAB[22]

Frequent medication and preventative measures such as mosquito nets were denied. Even under the most hygienic conditions people die but here the medical efforts seemed almost ineffective. The nurses' friends started to die and had to be left in the yard for twenty-four hours until coffins were provided. The women guarded the bodies from vermin during the night. There was a service for each burial.

The internees did not allow these dismal occurrences to destroy their will to live nor their imagination. "But the Japs could not get us down. They hated the British. They could not understand why we went about smiling and singing at our work. They said we should be serious, for there was a war on!"[23] Christmas 1943 was not as elaborate as the previous one and was Malay style, made from scraps saved for days, but entertainments in the new year did not lag. The six hundred women of different nationalities (twenty-six in all), three-quarters of whom were of Dutch extraction and one-quarter British, sang their traditional songs but these were eventually exhausted. A uniting musical form, a vocal orchestra, was devised by Mrs Chambers and Miss Dryburgh. Miss Dryburgh wrote the music in four parts representing the violin, viola, cello and double bass and the women who were interested "hummed" or "oohed" pieces by Tchaikovsky, Beethoven, Brahms, Debussy and Dvorak. They practised in the Dutch kitchen (frequently on stools as they were too weak to stand) and in small groups as the guards prohibited the internees from congregating in large groups. Three of the thirty members, Jeffrey, Trotter and Syer, were Australian nurses. From her diary Jeffrey remembers, "To sit on logs or stools or tables in the crude attap-roofed kitchen, with only one light, and then to be lifted right out of that atmosphere with this music is a sheer joy. It is so easy to forget one is a prisoner." The first performance was on 27 December 1943 and they continued these despite Japanese efforts to stop them. The Japanese also tried to prevent their card playing and other entertainment. The women had not expected so much beauty and even the Japanese stopped to listen. It helped renew the inmates' sense of human dignity, of being stronger than the enemy.

On April Fool's Day 1944 a military regime took command. The internees were promised extra bed space, more food and more work. In Jeffrey's words:

We are women and children and should do more work because
after the war we'll have to as [the] men will be too tired —
heaven help us — we can't work harder than we slog now — we
light (eventually) a fire to cook on — with this wet sappy wood
— no flame, and honestly sit from 7 a.m. till 12 noon blowing
the whole time and then all I've cooked is a small dish of tempi
[a slice made of curd and mung beans] and ubi [like tapioca]
and rice — spoonful of each — no wonder we look like walking
skeletons.

All the manual tasks were done by the women, including chopping tree trunks which were running with
rubber latex and covered with leaves, with one blunt
axe rostered for the whole camp. Completely removed
from the Allied men and outside information, the
women were required to respect the Japanese.

Military rule gave the appearance of being more
orderly as camp life was monitored and distinct
national groups were established at *tenko*. Captain
Seki was appointed commander, perhaps because he
had one eye that stared while the other was bloodshot,
physical attributes that may have accounted for his
demotion to looking after women. He left most of the
daily running of the camp to the Japanese and Javanese
guards, who were outnumbered by the internees but
were kept well-informed by some of the women (of
various nationalities) who were "girlfriends" of the
guards. Jeffrey described the guards: "Our protectors
are the best bunch of cut throats I've ever seen — oh
what an ugly race." The guards were known by their
nicknames and included "Ah Fat", second in command
and noted for his raucous demands, the "Student",
who was a sadist, "Lipstick Larry" who was violent
when women wore makeup, and "Seedling", who was
quite pleasant. Miss Syer observed:

74

The very dullest of them were sent with just sufficient of people who were capable of organizing things to guard the women, and the women were the lowest. We were a nuisance to them from first to last, and I think that was our great peril. And also the smaller group was in great danger. The more people that came into our camp as internees the more secure we felt. It's more difficult to get rid of a large group of people . . . I still don't understand why they didn't kill all of us earlier. It was a very lonely job and those people, those lowest of the low, were kicked around and they had been brutalized and they were brutal to us . . . We were the obstruction to their home and families.

Mrs Hinch, elected British camp commandant in July 1943, was able to reason with the Japanese in her dignified, serene manner.

Rations initially appeared to improve but thereafter they declined. Rations were weighed in the presence of the internees' rations officer, but when the sacks were opened the prisoners discovered that half the weight was stones and rubbish. Rice increased from half a cup per day per person to three-quarters of a cup and salt, sugar, tea and red palm oil were distributed. Weevily maize was a filling substitute for the vegetable rations that dropped by half, but was no replacement for the nutrition thus lost. In May they were given their first protein, fresh fish, and later live chickens. A guard showed some of the internees how to eat jungle foods so their normal rations were supplemented with non-poisonous wild vines, dahlias and most grasses. Seeds and young cuttings were issued and planted by the internees in their own plots; spinach, corn, tomatoes, tapioca and long beans flourished during the wet but not the dry season. Regular weighing of the internees, which the Japanese carefully documented, revealed that most of the British were around seven stone, a loss of two to three stone. In September 1944, James obtained a loan that enabled the nurses to buy extra food from the flourishing black market run by a few Indonesian guards. Loans were made at three hundred per cent interest to be paid after the war. Captain Seki stopped the black market in October 1944 with threats of severe punishment and solitary confinement.

A community kitchen was introduced in May 1944 so the British women followed the Dutch example and held meetings to form rice squads, wood cutters, water carriers, vegetable cutters, rations officers and bathroom cleaners. When the British changed arrangements, the Dutch assisted by cooking for the six hundred internees for twenty-four hours. The kitchen produced rice porridge at 7.00 a.m., black coffee at 10.00 a.m., a small bowl of rice with a dessertspoon of *kang kong* (a green which was like spinach and grew near gutters) and a teaspoon of *sambal* (a highly flavoured seasoning made from anything in the rations with chilli or curried stuffs) at midday, and at 5.00 p.m. another bowl of rice with a teaspoon of *kang kong* leaves and a dessertspoon of cucumber skin. Harper and Jeffrey built a small table, which they placed near their garden, and bought a serviette from a Dutch woman, so they could eat away from the crowd and "feel quite civilized". After dinner, sociable groups would form whilst they drank black coffee and smoked a cigarette of native tobacco — if they had any. The tobacco was so strong it had to be washed and dried several times before they smoked it. The internees constantly talked and dreamt food and copied recipes on bits of paper to take home. Jeffrey wrote in her diary on 30 April 1944: "Today I was so hungry that I could hardly walk. The first time it has hit me like this. I literally hadn't a thing to eat." For the nurses there was nothing worse than constant starvation. It was on the basis of these rations that the Japanese took advantage of female labour and saved themselves extra responsibility and cost.

Organized work parties were formed in May 1944 to tidy the camp and the overgrown gardens in the neighbourhood. Instead of axes or picks they were issued with *chungkals*, heavy native hoes which had an iron head and and a wooden handle, and weighed about twenty-two pounds. For some, these outdoor activities were a relief from camp chores, as it allowed them to exercise and vent their frustrations in physical exertion. For others, particularly the small women, the hoes were terrifying objects as they were almost too heavy to lift. At the height of the mid-year drought Captain Seki announced that there would be no more food; by September rice would be almost non-existent so the internees had to grow their own. They told the women they were "white coolies". Trotter said, "They used to tell us we'd have to work harder, we'd have less food, but there was always plenty of ground to bury us in . . . We were just an encumbrance really. I don't think they knew what to do with us."

The women worked in the gardens from 5.00 a.m. till 7.00 a.m. then 9.00 a.m. to 11.00 a.m. and again from 4.00 p.m. till 5.00 p.m. and carried water for the camp from 2.00 to 4.00 p.m. Sometimes they worked until 6.00 p.m. and during their break at 1.00 p.m. (the hottest part of the day) *tenko* was held. The sick were allowed shorter work hours but everyone was checked for work blisters. The centre of the camp had formed into hard clay but large garden beds for sweet potatoes and tapioca were dug. The wells were almost dry by July and the tap about a quarter of a mile outside the camp was only allowed to trickle for a couple of hours, usually in the middle of each day. From this the women, children and babies derived their water ration of a five pound butter tin per person per day. The water priorities were in descending order — the Japanese baths (twice daily), Japanese kitchen purposes, the gardens the internees tended, perhaps water for their kitchen, and occasionally water for bathing. Each Japanese threw at least four bucketsful over himself and their *tongs* had to be full. "Rasputin", a Japanese guard, refused to let the internees use the clean tap water for themselves and the dirty well or used water for the potatoes, despite the "Snake", another guard, ordering the woman to pour their sewerage over the plants as a punishment for being British. It was the British who protested against their treatment. The women took tins and discreetly poured clean water into them, and tipped water for the Japanese "accidentally" over themselves. The Japanese also ordered them to unload the ration trucks which sometimes had at least fifty heavy sacks. As Jeffrey said, the Japanese "do loathe us and get so mad when we chat brightly and organize a system to make the job easier". For their efforts the internees were infrequently paid wages despite promises of regular pay. In May 1944 they received their first wage, four guilders and fifty cents each, but in July this was replaced with a "bank account" of three bananas, a small piece of green pineapple (the tops were used as scrubbing brushes) and a cup of sugar, but normal rations were reduced.

As well as their manual tasks and nursing, most of the nurses maintained their money-making activities until 1945. For instance, Sylvia Muir minded a Dutch child, Florence Trotter cut hair and with Jessie Blanch washed clothes for the Dutch. Blanch also sewed buttonholes for an English friend. Joyce Tweddell (who constantly suffered from dysentery) sold her chillies for triple the price, and Betty Jeffrey raised her haircutting prices from ten to twenty cents but did not charge those who could not afford the service. Jeffrey and Harper also made foodstuffs to sell. Hannah and Simons found that their hats were not earning enough so they did sewing for the Dutch, such as making their mattresses into manageable sizes to carry when they moved, did the Dutch heavy work, sold cotton and performed various other jobs. At the next camp they had a cooking service for the hospital patients. Jeffrey recalled: "They never charge our own girls to hot up their food because they say 'you are in the family'." Physically the nurses had just enough energy for their own particular jobs. It was not always possible to rationalize their ill-health with the situation of some of the wealthier people who could afford extras.

The remaining Dutch and Germans were interned which temporarily cheered the British with hopes of an end to the war. Jeffrey retired from the shop and rations committee in July 1944, after "too many arguments with fat Germans about the distribution of things". Miss Netta Smith, a civilian nurse from Scotland who was also a hard worker in the camp, recalled that the Australian nurses "were very good and worked very hard". Trotter remembered:

> Some people in the camp, it didn't happen to our girls, said they had never worked like that in their lives and they had never eaten food like that in their lives and they weren't going to start now. Well you either ate it or you died. I remember one of the Dutch women saying to us after we'd been out in a party where you had to chop down the trees (I'd never had an axe in my hands before) . . . She said that's all right for you Australians you're used to this sort of thing . . . Some people do have that, they're not going to live like that and they don't live, they die.

Jeffrey expressed the nurses' exasperation in her diary in July 1944:

> One thing internment has taught me anyway is not to believe anything or anybody — nice outlook. I should say we were hardly worth rescuing from this — of the 218 British here there are not more than say twenty worth rescuing, the others are the world's worst shockers, oh the slum cats and fish wives and prostitutes and spies . . . give me a good old Aussie anytime.

This did not stop the Australians making friends nor keep them from having interests. The nationalities had to mix; they had the same difficulties and they helped each other to survive. The "rich" provided jobs for the "poor". They lived day by day with the hope of tomorrow.

All nationalities were united in hatred of their captors. Some of the civilian women could not believe that they were not due for leave as no white woman could be left for longer than three years in the tropics! Moreover they found it humiliating to bow to the Japanese. The nurses found it tiresome, but they were used to taking orders and had a disciplined nursing training. If the lines were crooked, or a woman smirked or did not bow, even if she did not see the guard, she would be slapped, prodded with a bayonet, kicked or beaten and made to stand in the boiling sun without a hat. The internees, however, discovered the peculiar temperaments of their guards and acted accordingly. Although the nurses preferred to remain inconspicuous they felt defiant until the final year. Group punishments were inflicted so any action an individual took had to be dissociated from the others. Ada Syer recalled this incident:

> I hadn't been out of hospital very long with very bad malaria and we had to go out to work with *chungkals* . . . We were lining up to be counted before we went out. Against the wall there was one pick and I went over and lifted it and it was very light. I thought if I'm going to work today I'm taking that pick. I was terrified of the *chungkal* . . . that I'd drop it on my head. The leader of this working group came up to me and said, "You know what you're doing" and I said, "Yes" and "You know what the consequences could be" and I said, "I won't involve the other women. I'll say you've been very nasty to me, meaning I'd defied the generals, the leader and the whole group" . . . He [the guard] came along and very slowly he looked up at me and I looked right past his ear . . . Through the interpreter he wanted to know why I had a pick . . . So I bowed and I said, "I realize I have to work. Nippon has to be fed but I am small, the *chungkal* is too heavy, but I can work very well with a pick (having no intention to work at all)." The group

81

leader told him and looked to him, shrugged her shoulders and I could understand enough to say that she was saying I was an outcast in the group and they'd done their best to make me behave and they couldn't do anything with me. He looked me in the eye and said in English, "You will work hard. I will watch." So I bowed very low and out we went and he watched. Anyway I did what I had to do. And the next day on the working party there were all picks — I accomplished something! That was defiance that paid off but I was very frightened . . . That was in the third year, not the fourth year, that was terrible. We were all so weakened . . . not many of us would've survived that year.

Raymont, one of the most delicate nurses, and Staff Nurse Valrie Smith were accused of damaging military property (by Rasputin) and forced to stand in the sun without hats, despite proof that Raymont had a heart condition and attempts by the others to protect her. She fainted.

The guards were not all cruel. Some had been educated in America and England and were sympathetic as they knew how the internees lived normally; others who were Christians talked to the internees and said they were "sorry", and others would talk of their families whom they missed. Moreover, as most of them were short they appeared to be afraid of tall women. They could also be surprisingly obtuse — if they were looking for the rush bags the fish came in they would not think to look at the hats the women wore. They covertly punished the women, however, by the lack of humanitarian treatment, poor living conditions and by restricting communication. Red Cross parcels were not distributed and mail was withheld.

The International Red Cross Committee (IRCC) had

Australian nurses on arrival in Singapore, February 1941. (Courtesy of Australian War Memorial)

Theatre facilities at the 2/10th Australian General Hospital, Malacca. From left: Sisters E. Moriarty and I. Ralston, and Staff Nurses D. Elmes (shot on Banka Island, 1942) and V. Haig. (Courtesy of Mrs F. Syer)

The Queensland nursing staff of the 2/10th Australian General Hospital in 1941. From left (front): Sister I. Ralston, Staff Nurse C. Oxley (POW), Matron O. Paschke (drowned 1942), Staff Nurses F. Trotter (POW), J. Blanch (POW), and E. Calnan (drowned 1942); (back): Staff Nurses J. Tweddell (POW), and C. Delforce (POW), Sister P. Mittelheuser (POW, died 1945), and Staff Nurses I. Grigg and M. Adams. (Courtesy of Australian War Memorial)

2/4th Casualty Clearing Station nurses, 1941: Staff Nurse D. Gardam (died Banka Island 1945), Sister E. M. Hannah (POW), and Matron I. Drummond (shot Banka Island 1942). (Courtesy of Australian War Memorial)

2/4th Casualty Clearing Station nursing staff, 1942. From left (front): Staff Nurse D. Gardam (POW, died 1945), Matron I. Drummond (shot Banka Island 1942), Sister E. M. Hannah (POW); (back): Staff Nurses E. Dorsch (drowned 1942), B. Willmott (shot Banka Island 1942), W. Raymont (POW, died 1945), Sister E. Balfour-Ogilvy (shot Banka Island 1942) and Staff Nurse P. Farmaner (shot Banka Island 1942). The photographer Sergeant-Major J. D. Emmett became a POW after the surrender of Singapore. He hid the film in Changi, and had it printed after the war. (Courtesy of Australian War Memorial)

Trying out the trenches in Malaya: Staff Nurses J. Blanch and F. Trotter. (Courtesy of Mrs F. Syer)

Wartime precautions: tin hat, gas mask and kitbag. These members of the 2/10th Australian General Hospital were prepared for war. (Courtesy of Mrs F. Syer)

Outside the 2/10th Field Ambulance Hospital, Rabaul, 1941. From left: Orderly Corporal D. Wells, Staff Nurses D. Keast and M. Anderson, with infant, and Orderly Corporal L. Hudson. (Courtesy of Mrs M. Morris-Yates)

The Bund Hotel in Yokohama, Japan, where the Army nurses captured in Rabaul were first quartered. (Courtesy of Mrs M. Morris-Yates)

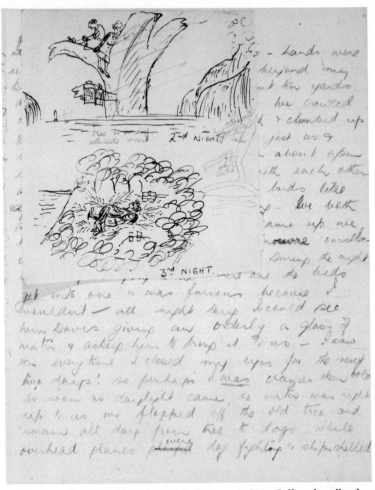

In the diary she kept while a POW, Staff Nurse A. Betty Jeffrey describes her experiences after the *Vyner Brooke* sank in Banka Strait, 1942. (Courtesy of Australian War Memorial)

The British kitchen at the women's camp, Palembang, drawn by Margaret Driver in pencil, 1944, 14.6 x 20.1 cm. (Courtesy of Australian War Memorial)

The hospital at the women's camp, Palembang, drawn by Sister Paula in pencil and violet pencil, 1945, 11.9 x 14.5 cm. (Courtesy of Australian War Memorial)

Japanese. facts.

Dear Mollie - my diary has been lost, it was written on Singapore each day until Monday 9th February 1942 when some of our girls left for home very suddenly - an hours notice, on a Hospital Ship, not our own, Chinese I believe by Wednesday things were getting very warm, awhile we were having breakfast at 6.45am, Matron was informed that our hospital was surrounded + we looked like being taken prisoner. There was no panic, we finished our meal, put on our red capes & with a small weekend suitcase, plus great coats & hats, we went across the tennis courts to the hospital & got on with the work. About 10 am word came for about thirty (?) sisters to go at once & make a dash for it - poor Matron, what a choice to have to make!! however, in her usual manner, the girls were named & off they went, hardly anyone saw them go as we were flat out receiving wounded & more wounded. Being constantly shelled, bombed at very close quarters - we were facing Bukit Timah Road - the main road down the island & this was constantly bombed for days on end.

Staff Nurse A. Betty Jeffrey's diaries were kept throughout captivity despite the fear of discovery. The 1944 entries show the effects of the paper crisis. (Courtesy of Australian War Memorial)

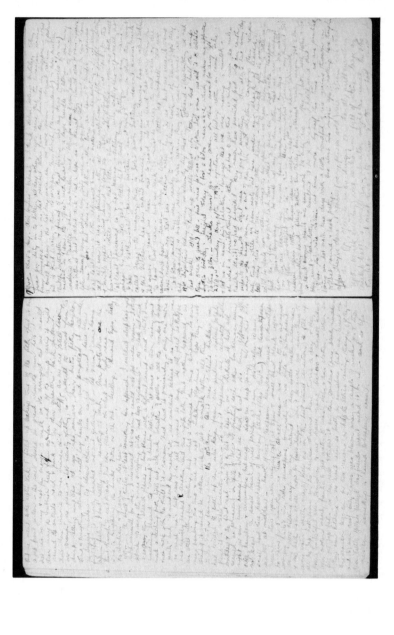

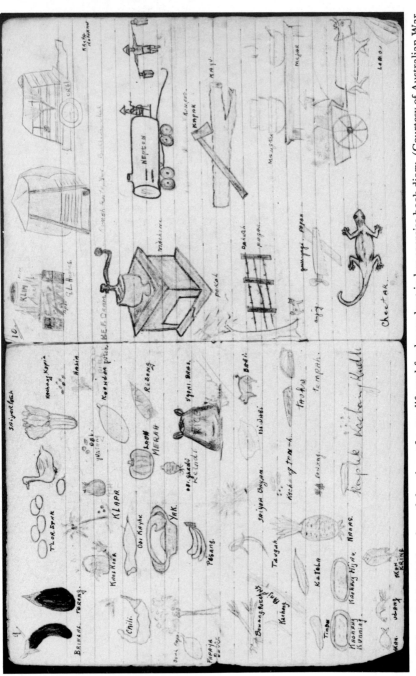

Staff Nurse Sylvia Muir's coloured drawings of camp life and food were kept in her exercise book diary. (Courtesy of Australian War

Food, food food: pages from a recipe book compiled by Staff Nurse Wilma Oram during captivity. (Courtesy of Australian War Memorial)

Teach yourself Malay: extracts from a notebook kept by Staff Nurse Wilma Oram. (Courtesy of Australian War Memorial)

Camp chores, from the diary of Sylvia Muir. (Courtesy of Australian War Memorial)

After their release, most of the nurses handed over their personal effects to the allied authorities, on the understanding that they were to be fumigated. Unfortunately their things were destroyed, resulting in the loss of many personal and historical records. Only a few of the nurses refused to part with their property, and were later able to donate it to the Australian War Memorial.

Felt pincushion decorated with felt and feathers, made in camp by Staff Nurse Wilma Oram.

Beret crocheted with a fencing-wire hook.

Cotton socks knitted in camp with pieces of fencing wire.

Appliqued straw-matting fan made in camp.

Valda Godley, a civilian interned with the nurses in Sumatra, died in the men's camp and left her personal effects to Staff Nurses Wilma Oram and Vivian Bullwinkel. Oram inherited a toothbrush, a long red evening gown which Sister Jean Ashton remodelled into a short daydress, and a red short-sleeved cotton blouse.

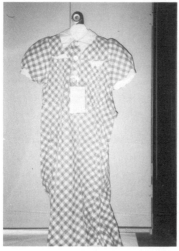 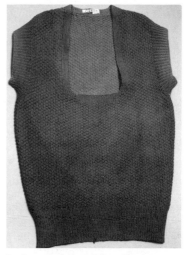

Red and white cotton dress made by Wilma Oram from material issued in camp.

Red vest knitted by Oram, considerably faded at the back from the intense heat as she worked in the gardens.

Staff Nurse Sylvia Muir's floral nightgown, made from voile issued while she was a POW in Sumatra, rated a place in her notebook diary and was far too beautiful to wear! (Courtesy of Australian War Memorial)

Spring Song

A Romance comes true
To live to meet life eager & unafraid, to refuse none
of its challenges, to evade none of its responsibilities, to
go forth daily in a gay & adventurous heart. To encounter
its risks to overcome its difficulties & to seize its opportunities with both hands.

Small piece of embroidery depicting the surroundings of the Palembang POW camp. (Courtesy of Australian War Memorial)

Palm matting purse made in camp. The women saw very little of the Japanese occupation money shown here. (Courtesy of Australian War Memorial)

1942

The Camp Choral Society

presents

Two Concerts on the 24th & 31st October respectively,

at 8pm in House No 7.

(By courtesy of the Australian Nursing Sisters)

Additional items by

The Dutch members of the choir

Margaret Dryburgh

Margery Jennings

Dorothy MacLeod

Ena Murray

Norah Chambers

Due to lack of space it is requested that houses Nos 1 to 7 attend the concert on the 24th October, and houses Nos 8 - 14 attend the concert on the 31st.

Accommodation will be limited inside the room but the overflow can be seated in the garden, if they bring seats.

No children by request.

Invitation to the Camp Choral Society concert. (Courtesy of Australian War Memorial)

The Captive's Hymn, with music and words composed by Margaret Dryburgh, became a source of great strength to many of the prisoners. It was appreciated not only for its spiritual message, but also for its beauty as a musical composition. (Courtesy of Australian War Memorial)

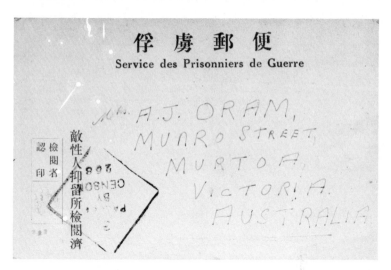

Both sides of a POW postcard sent by Staff Nurse Wilma Oram to her family in 1943. (Courtesy of Australian War Memorial)

TO:-
Name VX 58783 W. Oram
Mr. Mrs. Miss Women's Internment
Camp PALEMBANG
Country SUMATRA

FROM:-
Name MR A.J. ORAM
Street MUNRO STREET
Suburb MURTOA
Town
State VICTORIA AUSTRALIA

Date 25-12-43.

DEAREST WILMA. RECEIVED CARD AFTER MANY
MONTHS. LANCE WOUNDED, RECOVERING. PA AND I ARE
WELL. PATTIE IN THE SERVICES. STILL IN OLD HOME
MRS BULL. MELBOURNE. SICK.
MOTHER.

TO:-
Name VX 58783 W. Oram
Mr. Mrs. Miss Women's Internment
Camp PALEMBANG
Country SUMATRA

FROM:-
Name Mrs A.J. Oram.
Street 99 Palmer Street
Suburb Portland.
Town
State Victoria AUSTRALIA

Date 13-2-44.

My darling Wilma.
Hope well, Pa playing
bowls. Lance Recovering. Staying here
for a while. Nearly twelve months since we
had a card from you.
Heaps love.
Mum.

FROM
Name Mrs. A. J. Oram   Town MURTOA
Street Munro   State VICTORIA AUSTRALIA

Date 24 November 1944

Dear Willie,

            Had news that you are working
and well. Praying that you are still in
good health and spirits. Everyone of us
are well.

            Love.

            Mother.

News from home! Official postcards that families used to send messages to prisoners of war. (Courtesy of Australian War Memorial)

Death and despair: Staff Nurse Betty Jeffrey's diary. (Courtesy of Australian War Memorial)

Survivors in Singapore, 1945. From left (front): Nesta James, Mavis Hannah, Jessie Simons, Iole Harper and Betty Jeffrey; (back): Florence Trotter, Christian Oxley, Eileen Short, Veronica Clancy, Beryl Woodbridge, Cecilia Delforce, Jess Doyle, Ada Syer, Violet McElnea, Jean Ashton, Valrie Smith, Pat Blake and Wilma Oram. (Courtesy of Australian War Memorial)

Australian nurses captured in Rabaul and held in Yokohama, photographed on their release. (Courtesy Mrs M. Morris-Yates)

In Manila after their release from Japan, 1945: Staff Nurse D. Keast, Sister K. Parker, and Staff Nurses M. Cullen and L. Whyte. Only Parker was able to wear her carefully saved uniform into freedom. (Courtesy of Australian War Memorial)

In Manila after their release from Japan, 1945. From left (front): J. McLellan (AN), J. Christopher (M), D. Maye (AN), E. Jones (an American school teacher from the Aleutian Islands), M. Green (M), Staff Nurse L. Whyte, Staff Nurse D. Keast; (back): G. Kruger (AN), A. Beaumont (AN), J. McGowan (AN), D. Beale (M), D. Wilson (M), J. Oldroyd-Harris (AN), M. Goss (AN), K. Bignell (civilian housewife), Staff Nurse M. Cullen, Sister K. Parker. (AN: administrative nurse; M: Methodist missionary) (Courtesy of Australian War Memorial)

In Manila, 1945. From left (front): J. McLellan, J. Christopher, E. Jones, M. Green, L. Whyte; (back): J. McGowan, D. Beale, D. Maye, D. Wilson, J. Oldroyd-Harris, M. Goss. (Courtesy of Australian War Memorial)

Emotional family welcome for Sister Kay Parker, home at last, 1945. (Courtesy of Australian War Memorial)

Back in Australia: Sister Kay Parker and Staff Nurses Lorna Whyte, Mavis Cullen and Daisy Keast. (Courtesy of Australian War Memorial)

Arrival in Australia, 1945: Kay Parker, Lorna Whyte, Daisy Keast and Mavis Cullen. (Courtesy of Australian War Memorial)

Postcard of the 2/14th Australian General Hospital in Singapore, 1945. (Courtesy of Mrs F. Syer)

Australian nurses photographed on board the hospital ship *Manunda* with floral tributes and gifts after their arrival in Fremantle. From left (front): Christian Oxley, Jean Greer, Beryl Woodbridge, Florence Trotter; (middle): Eileen Short, Jessie Blanch, Valrie Smith, Violet McElnea, Betty Jeffrey, Colonel A. M. Sage, unknown, Nesta James, Pat Blake, Janet Gunther, Mavis Hannah, Jess Doyle, Cecilia Delforce, Iole Harper, unknown, Vivian Bullwinkel, Sylvia Muir and Joyce Tweddell; (back): V. Haig, Wilma Oram, and Jean Ashton. The nurse obscured behind Iole Harper and the two marked unknown are Jessie Simons, Ada Syer, and Veronica Clancy, but the author has been unable to ascertain who is who. (Courtesy of Mrs F. Syer)

An exuberant welcome from Sister D. M. Wright to Staff Nurses Florence Trotter and Violet McElnea, 1945. (Courtesy of Mrs F. Syer)

Flowers galore! From left: Cecilia Delforce, Sylvia Muir and Veronica Clancy, in 1945. (Courtesy of Australian War Memorial)

Staff Nurse Vivian Bullwinkel, the sole survivor of the Banka Island massacre, pictured with her mother on her arrival in Australia in 1945. (Courtesy of Australian War Memorial)

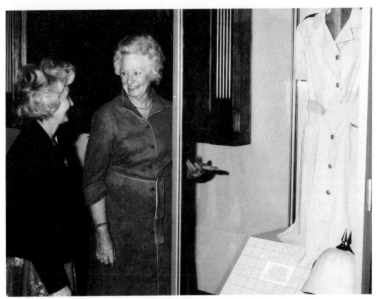

Mrs Vivian Statham (née Bullwinkel) pointing to her uniform donated to the Australian War Memorial. (Courtesy of Australian War Memorial)

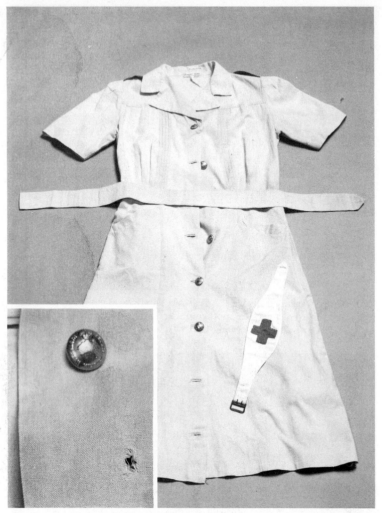

"Pioneer" service uniform, Collins Street, Melbourne: Vivian Bullwinkel's uniform and Red Cross armband. Even her name tag remains on the collar. (Courtesy of Australian War Memorial)

(Inset): Vivian Bullwinkel's uniform shows the bullethole made when she was wounded in the Banka Island massacre, of which she was the sole survivor. (Courtesy of Australian War Memorial) delegates in Tokyo, Shanghai and Hong Kong, but the Japanese government did not permit the appointment or recognition of delegates in other Japanese-controlled places. Local agents of the IRCC residing in Singapore and Bangkok could make limited purchases of relief for POWs and internees with funds provided by national Red Cross societies, but they were not officially recognized. Swiss consular representatives were also able to make limited purchases, and relief supplies were sent by the national Red Cross societies. In October 1944 the nurses in Sumatra received one American Red Cross parcel, the only such delivery during their three and a half years of captivity. Each person recieved twenty-two cigarettes, one inch of chocolate that was growing fur, half a cup of powdered milk, four small loaves of sugar, a small packet of soup powder between three, and a half pound tin of jam, a small tin of meat and one of salmon between fifteen, an inch of cheese, a spoonful of coffee essence and a spoonful of butter. The Japanese kept most of the boxes of milk, butter and cheese and all medical supplies.

The nurses were shocked when a Japanese officer told them that Japanese submarines had been in Sydney Harbour, but this like other news was never substantiated, although they were given bananas as a present when Australia returned the soldiers' ashes to Japan. Unlike the men in Changi these women had no constant source of information. During captivity the Australians received five batches of mail. The first mail, mostly dated 1942 and 1943, arrived in August 1944 after being delayed by the guards for three months. Jeffrey wrote: "After living an hour of terrific suspense I at last saw a letter addressed to me in mother's own handwriting — I just went cold all over, it was so familiar after all this awfulness and filth and dreadful conditions and terrible people." Some of the nurses did not get letters, and three of the nurses learnt of the death of a parent. Harper, Smith and Syer received no mail during the war, despite their parents' efforts. They were also allowed to write their second letter home but no mention could be made that they were hungry, thirsty and worked hard, nor of the impending move back to Muntok. The move came months after the first Allied bombing raids on the oil refineries close by. Unlike the guards the women were given no protection and were not allowed to illuminate the hospital or erect a red cross.

"Plenty Room in the Cemetery"

In October 1944, the internees were moved back to Muntok on Banka Island to a superficially superior camp. They left in four contingents and travelled in badly ventilated boats, many arriving so ill that the Japanese virtually had to carry them off. The last contingent included the hospital staff and patients; their boat became uncontrollable during the rough weather. About 120 more Dutch, Indo-Dutch and Indonesians were added to the camp during the move.

The new gravel hilltop location was clean and airy. There were six huts capable of housing 140 people with sufficient bed space and a new rush mat on which to sleep. There were three large kitchens, nine cemented clean wells and a creek nearby. The only apparent drawback was the lavatories, cement pits next to the kitchen. The original sanitary squad could not cope with the outflow from the drains and pits so Harper, Bullwinkel, Oram and Ashton helped them and earned eighty cents a day from a camp fund. They worked double time so they did not lose money if they were down with fever. In these surroundings the death rate escalated.

The emergency health situation released fourteen of the Australian and British nurses from camp chores so they could join the nuns in the hospital. All but one of the numerous Dutch civilian nurses stopped nursing. "Banka Fever", a virulent new disease and probably a form of cerebral malaria, originating from the creek, affected all nationalities and ages. This, with beri-beri, malaria and dysentery, was the predominant disease. At times seventy-five per cent of the camp of around seven hundred were sick. The Australians were periodically affected by these diseases; their weight fell and coordination diminished, but they were expected to assist in the hospital even when they were sick. Medical teams worked day and night and when there was no light they worked with an oil lamp. The hospital was better organized and Ashton and Sister Reynelda (a nun) acted as joint matrons of the hospital.

Lack of medication and equipment radically reduced the effect of the medical care; no surgical operations could be performed. The Japanese contributed a small bottle of about one hundred quinine tablets every five to six weeks for the whole camp, or quinine bark which caused severe dysentery. Those who were friendly with the natives received supplies more often. A rule was established that a member of staff had to watch the patient swallow the tablet, as a single tablet commanded a price equivalent to three pounds sterling on the black market. In November they received eleven guilders each from the American Red Cross: "What a relief this is! Hospital and camp expenses are terrific; we pay 50 cents for a green mango and 60 cents for an indifferent banana. Jap rations alone would not keep anyone alive."[24]

Around Christmas the situation became very serious with people dying every day; mothers who had starved themselves for their children were particularly affected. "Some people who had so much to live for, married women with husbands interned, and children at school, just gave up and said they could not go on living indefinitely in this fashion."[25] Syer and Hannah both recalled that after severe illness neither wanted to eat, and had to force themselves. Syer remembered:

At one stage I had repeated attacks of malaria and I came to the state where I thought I cannot eat another bowl of rice. I knew if I didn't eat the rice when it came, the next time it came I'd have no choice — I'd just refuse it and in those circumstances you cannot afford to turn away any source of nourishment whatsoever. So I had a gold watch which was a keepsake which stopped when I jumped into the water off our ship. I'd worn it into internment without ever thinking of it being of ultimate value. I hadn't turned that into cash beforehand — about three years — I had reached that stage I thought now I've got to have something else to eat. In desperation I gave this watch to somebody who had contacts outside the wire, on the black market, and I got an egg. It was none too fresh but I ate it. And the next time when the rice came around I ate it. So I think the will to live made me make the right choice but I wasn't conscious of it. It was something I had to do.

The nurses, despite their care for each other, also died. On 8 February 1945 Wilhelmina Raymont, aged thirty-three years, died of cerebral malaria. She had suffered repeated attacks of malaria and had never recovered from her punishment in September 1944, which had kept her hospitalized for some time after. Soon afterwards Staff Nurses Irene Singleton and Pauline Hempsted (both thirty-six) died from malnutrition and beri-beri, and Dorothy Gardam (thirty-four) died from malaria, although all four were inflicted with the triad of diarrhoea, malaria and deficiency diseases. Singleton and Staff Nurse Rubina Freeman, who died later, almost starved themselves selling food to earn money for the future. Emaciated beyond recognition, Singleton had pleaded for more food the day she died. Her dry humour was remembered and missed. Hempsted was an extremely hard worker which assuredly hastened her death. She apologized just before she died for taking so long. Gardam, always frail and nervous, died suddenly after a long illness. She had received no letters and did not know her mother had died in 1942. The Australian nurses gave their dead full military funerals and wore their tattered uniforms. Jeffrey recorded: "It made the Japs sit up; they even stood to attention and removed their caps as it went past their quarters, a thing they had never done before."

The Australian nurses, as they were known, remained a strong and cohesive group who were a source of strength to themselves as well as to the other internees. If decisions were made they were made together. Simons said, "We were like sisters of a family. Of course we did not always see eye to eye, but what sisters do?" When there had been more hope, divisive factors in the camp had been more evident, but when everyone was ill they had to combine in the relentless struggle of survival. Syer observed:

Oh we had squabbles but we had fewer squabbles as time went on. We were down to the very basic form of life, there was less to quarrel about and we were tired. It didn't mean we didn't discuss things and argue but we did it with less irritation. We had peeled off so many aspects of civilization by that time, that we were down to the core of things and the core of things is fairly simple.

The women endeav ared to keep as optimistic as possible but the constant and debilitating effects of malnutrition and disease caused weakness, memory loss, lack of concentration and lassitude. "No more concerts, or charades or sing songs; when the day's work is done people go off to their beds and lie there until morning." As it was observed in some of the men's camps, religion seemed to have no enhanced appeal where there was sickness and death. Christmas celebrations lacked the enthusiasm of former years. There were no presents, not even cards as they had run out of paper. Miss Dryburgh held a short service but most of the women could not sing as their voices were gone or very weak. The voice choir, which had given the internees so much joy, stopped in early 1945 when half of its members had died.

Nothing was known of the successes of the Allies, only the relentless battle to survive. There were one or two, sometimes three, funerals a day among their own acquaintances. The internees did not have to do the manual work as at the men's camp but they had to arrange funerals, dig the graves and help the young boys and guards make the coffins. The two commandants, Mother Laurentia and Mrs Hinch, insisted that the Japanese provide small wooden crosses which Mrs

Chambers and Mrs Audrey Owen (a New Zealander who had lived in Malaya) inscribed.

> I'm pleased to see our dear Mr Curtin (if he is still P.M.) did not have the nerve to send us a Xmas message of cheer and to keep smiling for the third time — perhaps the smile has been dashed from his own face — 31 of our 32 now have malaria very badly . . . we are just hoping and praying for our freedom and home soon or [we] will be messes for the rest of our lives.[26]

The prisoners were again moved in April 1945, but the customary repatriation rumours were outweighed by weariness, sickness and apprehension. Again the nurses were divided. Jeffrey recalled, "We hate being separated like this, even if it is only temporarily." As usual they travelled in their remnants of uniforms and Red Cross armbands in case anyone perchance saw them. Despite repeated pleas the Japanese insisted that the second of the three contingents to leave the camp should be the hospital staff and patients, some of whom were gravely ill and had only a few hours to live. Those nurses who could carried the stretcher cases onto the boat, despite the presences of dozens of Japanese soldiers who watched with "horrified" faces but made no move to assist. James described the journey:

> It was the same frightful boat on which we had come over previously. The hospital staff and the patients were put on the deck without any covering from the sun at all. The remainder of the people were put in the hold, which was even worse. The crowding on the ship was completely disgraceful. There were no sanitary arrangements at all. At the time people were suffering severely from diarrhoea — practically everybody that had been in camp.[27]

A Dutchwoman died on the pier and an Englishwoman was buried at sea. Jeffrey wrote, "That burial was a nightmare." They were loaded onto trains and the stretcher cases into cattle trucks. Several died before they left the station. James continued:

> We remained that night at Palembang with all the shutters down, in the stifling heat, and sanitary conditions ghastly. [There were no lavatories and excreta could only be ejected out of a sliding hatch high in the walls.] Next day we set off and were allowed between stations to have the shutters up a few inches. The odour of sweating humanity became terrible . . . We arrived at Loebok Linggau having lost several more patients on the way. These . . . were left for several hours dead in the vans. Some were carried more or less strung under the train.

The nurses who were fit enough attended to the sick. James said, "The next morning, quite early, we were taken by truck to our camp, almost at the stage of collapse." Winnie Davis, who was already there, had saved some food for them. Miss Dryburgh was one of those who never recovered from the trip and her contribution was sorely missed after she died on 21 April 1945.

The new location, Belalau Camp near Loebok Linggau, was hidden in a rubber plantation abandoned and wrecked by its former Dutch inhabitants. A boundary of barbed wire and rubber trees confined the camp, which was split by a creek. One bank of the creek was elevated and about six hundred female internees, including eighteen Australian nurses (who were again reluctantly separated), were housed in badly built *attap* huts swarming with bugs and lice, with wooden *bali-balis* (beds) over concrete or mud floors. On the lower side were British and Dutch community kitchens and their staff, a one-roomed cottage that housed the Charitas nuns and a smaller one-roomed house which accommodated ten Australian nurses and had an iron roof in adequate condition and a concrete floor. They each had twenty-two inches of bed space. There were no bathrooms so they used the creek in full view of the guards whom they had learnt to ignore as their clothes barely covered them anyway. The creek supplied their water but the eight lavatories were built over the creek, which became even more polluted with refuse from the kitchen and the Japanese quarters further upstream.

The major obsessions of food, water and disease plagued this their last camp as it had every other. The rice ration was reduced but they did receive more vegetables, though these were dumped outside the camp for three or four days to rot before the internees could collect them, and this caused indigestion. The inmates supplemented the vegetables with ferns and grasses that grew on the creek banks. The black market functioned under increasing difficulties and charged exorbitant prices. When they had enough energy the women tended their own vegetable patches. At Muntok they had eaten goat, turtle eggs and turtle soup, but here their diet extended to a tiny monkey (each person received two pieces the size of dice), deer and bear. Red palm oil was available in greater quantities for cooking and it was also found to be a soothing skin medication as well as a useful oil for homemade rag lamps, since there were no other lights. The cooking and distribution of food and the collection of water posed problems for the women on the high bank, who found it too exhausting to make regular trips down and back. The cooks were neither well enough nor the wood supply plentiful enough to cook more than once a day, so the kitchen staff cooked the rice at 10.00 a.m. for distribution to the internees, who supplemented their rations at their houses during the day. Outside the camp were banana and pawpaw trees but the internees were punished if they took any fruit. It was too difficult to steal bunches so they took the banana flowers which were a great delicacy when curried, as were the banana skins dried and fried. Despite a wood shortage they were not allowed to collect wood, so some of the internees attended funerals just to obtain some outside the camp.

Rather than expend their energy the women on the upper bank did not bathe and sometimes went without water for other purposes. Their coconut toothbrushes had rapidly worn out and they used ash for toothpaste. Simons occasionally hired an internee to carry water for her at forty cents a bucket but the woman soon weakened and the money ran out. The nurses had become used but not reconciled to using their boiled dirty bath water for other purposes and to never being able to clean themselves or their surroundings properly.

The ten Australian nurses on the lower side worked in the hospital and the others continued district nursing. The hospital had two wards, one with a cement floor and the other with an earthen floor that was frequently ankle-deep in mud and filth. The nurses could only work for an hour or two before they had to rest and volunteer aids were called to fill the duty roster. Jeffrey, one of the hospital nurses, wrote in her diary:

> Food comes in to camp alright, but it is for the workers (not nurses they don't "work" — they nurse and have to live on rations). The workers are mostly Indo-Dutch and Indonesians and big boys — they get sugar, cakes, bananas, rice, corn, vegetables, extra to rations. If one works in the kitchen one gets a dish full of rice. If one nurses, one gets nothing but insults, malaria and an empty tummy.

The district nurses also encountered difficulties as deficiency disease inhibited movement, but they each looked after about fifty women in huts throughout the camp. Those nurses who were too weak eventually stopped their nursing duties. Camp jobs were allocated on the basis of strength. When they asked for more food they were told "plenty room in the cemetery".

Each morning an estimate was required of the number of graves and coffins to be made, as women of all ages and nationalities died daily. The mortality rate was 37.1 per cent and one in four of the Australian nurses died. Four more nurses died during this period, one after official peace had been declared on 15 August 1945. Neither she nor the others knew. Staff Nurse Gladys Hughes died in May 1945, aged thirty-seven. The only New Zealander, she had done Public, Private and Bush Nursing in Australia before the war. She was a popular woman valued for her new cooking ideas. Like the other three she died from malaria, persistent diarrhoea and malnutrition. The women were oedematous and had gangrenous patches but they were conscious to the end. In the last few months many of the survivors also had nutritional oedema. Winnie Davis, one of the youngest nurses and always mindful of others, was thirty when she died after weeks of illness. Jeffrey mourned, "Win had so much to live for and wanted so badly to have six sons." Rubina Freeman died in August 1945 aged thirty-two. "Flo [Trotter] was on night duty and was terribly shaken, as we all were." Hannah wrote:

> By September 1945 I remained the sole surviving Sister of my unit [2/4th CCS], four were shot, two drowned and two [Gardam and Raymont] died in camp in 1945. One of these died a raving lunatic from cerebral malaria. I had begged the Commandant to give me anti-malarial medication, which they had withheld from Red Cross parcels; I was told there was plenty of room in the cemetery. He laughed, smacked my face and his guard hit me with his rifle. I bear the marks to this day.

Most of the nurses had lost around three stone, although some such as Tweddell, one of the youngest members aged twenty-nine, had lost nearly seven stone. Jeffrey discovered that by bending her elbows she could span her wrist and her upper arm with her finger and thumb. Some of the women who were not heavy before the war, however, weighed around eight stone, a drop of about two stone. Ashton and Oram, the youngest Australian nurse, frequently did double time in the hospital because there were always nurses ill with malaria. Three days after V.J. day, Pearl Mittelheuser died at the age of forty-one. She had worked hard as house captain and housekeeper. The will to live succumbed to unconquerable disease. The American Red Cross medical supplies, seen unpacked a year before, had not been distributed to the internees.

The women still managed to find something to laugh and talk about, but parties were held in small groups, with everyone bringing their own coffee and sugar; there were no camp activities as they had all become too weary. By May most of the women had drawn up wills countersigned by two witnesses which the Japanese and other internees respected. The British and Australians had very little to leave but the dead reclothed the living. Friendships were vitally important and developed between people from varying backgrounds. Simons recalled she became very sick with malaria and depressed after Hannah went into hospital with a weak heart and beri-beri; at this stage she was befriended by a Eurasian who provided company and helped cook. Her experience was not uncommon, although in civilian life it is unlikely such friendships would have existed. In primitive conditions with no escape from each other people could not have pretensions.

Throughout their captivity rumours of release abounded. The natives and "girlfriends" of the Japanese would tell optimistic tales but they were generally disbelieved. Nonetheless, in late May the internees celebrated the Allied victory over Germany (which they thought had occurred before Christmas) not long after the actual date of the unconditional surrender on 7 May 1945, but no news was certain. Apart from the release of more mail, an evening of superb music performed by a Japanese military band in May and the distribution of fourteen live pigs in July, camp life remained the same until late August. The letters from Australia appeared to be oblivious of a war and spoke of troops being "demobbed". A week before

Captain Seki announced that the war was over the children were allowed to visit their male relatives in the men's camp nearby. The women discovered whether their husbands, friends and brothers had died when the Japanese read out a long list of children who could not go. The guards looked noticeably forlorn and the Japanese "girlfriends" reported that war was over and that the interpreter had been crying for a week.

The official announcement on 24 August 1945 attracted only a small crowd, as most of the women thought it would as usual be bad news. Seki merely announced: "War is ended, Americano and English will be here in a few days. We are now all friends." Trotter said he looked as if he had been up all night. The internees were free, but too stunned to appreciate the import of the word — all Oram, Woodbridge, Tweddell, Muir and Ashton felt was relief. Simons sat under a rubber tree and cried for half an hour. Blanch did not believe it until there was plenty of food and clothing. Ashton pitied the parents of the nurses who had died, Hannah felt "very flat", and James was elated. That night weak-voiced renditions of "God Save the King" and the national songs of Holland were sung.

Life was the same until the next day when boxes of medical supplies, towels, wash-basins, mosquito nets and vegetables arrived in the camp. New supplies, including the long delayed Red Cross parcels, continued to arrive daily. The nurses creamed butter and sugar and ate until they were sick. A Japanese doctor came and took a great interest in the patients. Everything they had been short of was found in the Japanese stores, and the natives were eager to swap food for clothing (Japanese uniforms) that the Japanese gave the internees. Four back teeth on a gold bridge that Oxley had only just put on the black market to buy food were now returned. The Dutch government sent a message that it would send food and pay for it; "What a relief that is, after living on our wits, more or less, all this time, trying to earn money to buy miserable bits of food to keep body and soul together."[28] The Japanese efforts to call *tenko* were ignored.

The numb feeling Jeffrey experienced finally disappeared when the civilian men from a camp nearby arrived and took control. "Oh it was marvellous to see real men at last after seeing nothing but monkeys running around in khaki for three and a half years (and two weeks)." The men took over all the domestic and manual chores. Bullwinkel recalled feeling left out because the nurses had no men to look after them, but a Dutchman they had met when they were first taken prisoner at Muntok appointed himself as their cook. To their surprise the men treated them as ladies with civilized manners, rising when they entered the room.

On 7 September 1945 a small party from the Intelligence Headquarters of South-East Asia Command in Colombo, Ceylon, found the camp after hearing about the Banka Island massacre from one of the male survivors. Major G. Jacobs of the Royal Marines, in charge of the mission to locate camps and arrange rescue operations, arrived accompanied by two Australians, Sergeants Bates and Gillam. In his book *Prelude to the Monsoon*, Jacobs revealed that Japanese Command had not admitted to any more camps, but evidence given by prisoners at Palembang made him suspicious. When he confronted the Japanese they said a "mistake" had been made and there was still one more camp. Jacobs acted immediately and flew into Lahat then drove to the camp. Even on a cursory look he saw that it was in a "deplorable condition".[29] He described the conditions at Loebok Linggau as the worst he had encountered and was appalled by the state of the prisoners. They radioed Colombo for an air drop of food and medical supplies which arrived soon after. The following message was sent to Headquarters in Ceylon:

> Have encountered among 250 repeat 250 British female internees in Loebok Linggau camp Sister Nesta James and 23 other surviving members of Australian Army Nursing Services remnants of contingent AANS evacuated from Malaya in Vyner Brooke stop In view their precarious health suggest you endeavour arrange air transport direct to Australia from here soonest stop Am collecting particulars massacre of members AANS, on Banka Island for later transmission.[30]

Jacobs requested Headquarters to repeat this to the Australian ambassador in India and Army Headquarters in Melbourne. Despite these efforts the Australian nurses were found by the perseverance of journalists who heard their story from another source. The two Australians accompanying Jacobs were constantly questioned about world affairs. So much had changed; the nurses' information was hopelessly out of date.

Companionship and friendship were vital during captivity. The nurses had integrated within the internee community but their separate identity was not lost. They worked hard at their duties and their money-making ventures which assuredly hastened their deaths. Camp life diminished as the women suffered from the ill-effects of their treatment but the support the nurses gave each other, their sense of humour and their desire to return to Australia contributed to their determination to stay alive. The same tenacity and group identity was evident in the six Army nurses from Rabaul who had become POWs in Japan.

Rabaul to Yokohama

Unlike the Army nurses in Sumatra, the six captured in Rabaul became part of a group of nineteen mainly civilian internees, most of whom were Australian nurses. They were taken to Japan and for over three years had no communication with family and friends and virtually no contact with the local population, except for their guards who kept them under close scrutiny. Initially they received adequate treatment and led a leisurely existence, but after the first year conditions deteriorated. They were hungry, constantly suffered from the cold and only had a tiny community to use as a means to relieve the monotony.

After the Japanese took over in January 1942, the Army nurses had been determined to keep their hospital at the Vunapope mission functioning. Chaplain May, who had undertaken responsibility for the nurses, was taken away within twenty-four hours but Sister Kay Parker, who had been left in charge of the military hospital, obtained permission for the six nurses to tend their sick and wounded. Each day they were escorted by an armed naval guard to the native hospital, which was about a quarter of a mile from the main mission buildings and convent, but within mission grounds. There was very little food or drugs but the nuns at the convent and some of the nurses broke into the Burns Philp Store and stole food which they hid in the hospital. After a week the Japanese became more organized; they confiscated the food and drugs from the Army and civilians nurses but allowed the Army nurses to continue nursing. Captain Robertson, one of the medical officers, was caught and returned briefly to the Army hospital, but the nurses would not speak to him and the Australian soldiers wanted to treat him roughly. The nurses continued their efforts until 28 April 1942 when most of the men had recovered and been sent to the main POW camp in Rabaul. Staff Nurse Marjory Anderson, now Mrs Morris-Yates, said, "We knew having seen it in the hospital, even in the short time after capture and whilst we were still caring for our own soldiers, there were quite a few of those boys who turned their faces to the wall and just died, and we knew what had happened to those boys and it wasn't going to happen to us."

The Japanese assumed that the women were for the "pleasure" of the troops. The night after the Japanese arrived Eileen Callaghan awoke with a bayonet pressed against her cheek. A Japanese had forced the window, but when she called out and one of the other nurses turned on the light he went away. Instead of being hostile, the naval officers in charge invited the women to their officers' club in Rabaul but they declined the invitation. The women slept downstairs in the convent music room until the Japanese nocturnal wanderings forced them to sleep in the sacristy, sometimes on top of cupboards. The soldiers would lounge on their beds, demand music and entertainment, and would occasionally attempt to fondle and chase them. The nuns tried to protect them and a Seventh Day Adventist, Pastor E.M. Abbott, spent the first night sleeping across their doorway but he was taken away on 24 January 1942. For three weeks the Army nurses, except Callaghan who was a strict Catholic, slept with a phial of morphia to kill themselves if there was an attempted rape. These activities stopped when a boatload of Geisha girls arrived in late February. Despite the close proximity of the guards in the following years there were no more sexual advances.

After these initial weeks, the internees were mostly left alone by their guards. They did however have to show respect to their captors and bow every time a Japanese guard was present or incur punishment. The officers were generally bombastic and rank conscious, could speak some English and often seemed to dislike their prisoners. Parker endeavoured to impress them by using her honorary rank of Captain, but no concessions were made. They ignored the nurses' armbands and said they knew nothing about the Geneva Conventions or the Red Cross. Ironically, some of the guards who were only fourteen had thought they were going on a cruise and were frightened and homesick so the nurses comforted them and Lorna Whyte (the youngest Army nurse) taught a few to knit. One Japanese, a bank clerk educated in England, was friendly.

The women secretly kept in contact with the Australian soldiers who lived in a shed opposite the convent for a short while, and with the civilians who occasionally passed through the camp. Letters and parcels were delivered to the Australian officers in the township and the women also received mail. In March they were allowed to write a letter to their relatives which the Japanese said would be dropped over Port Moresby in a bombing raid. The nurses doubted this but the carefully censored letters were in fact dropped and received by at least the Keasts and the Andersons. Keast and Parker signed each other's names on their letters to double the chances of their parents' being informed of their safety.

Staff Nurse Daisy (Tootie) Keast to Keast family, 24 March 1942

My darlings,

By kind permission of the Japanese authorities I am able to write you a one-page letter. It's just one big thrill. I'm very well, having plenty of food, good accommodation . . . also able to continue my work. We are very lucky and realize it. How are you all at home? . . . It seems an age since I heard from you but we are hoping soon to be able to receive a letter. No need to say how much I think of you each day . . . please don't worry.

Tootie K. Parker

Until August 1945 this was the only news the parents had of their daughters. Only four of the six nurses, Anderson, Callaghan, Parker and Whyte, were reported "Missing, believed POW" on 5 March 1943.

The Mother Superior and nuns helped them feel as comfortable as possible, and apart from cooking there was little to do. The Army nurses' former cookboy brought them some of their clothes and belongings saved from their bomb-destroyed house. The Army, administrative and Methodist nurses and the civilian Mrs K. Bignell, who had formerly run a convalescent hospital for soldiers, now got to know each other, although they had not previously associated.

The women were still treated with suspicion. In June they were again lined up at gunpoint and the camp was given a surprise search at 5.00 a.m. The Japanese suspected the women of sending messages out of Rabaul and stood them in the sun for seven hours. They found nothing and left them unharmed. The next day the civilian clergy, three civilian doctors and numerous troops and civilians embarked on the *Montevideo Maru*. It was not marked to show it was carrying POWs and internees and was sunk by an American submarine off Luzon in the Philippine Islands on 1 July 1942, on its way to Japan. There were no survivors.

On 5 July 1942 the eighteen women internees were given short notice that they were to embark on an unmarked ship, the *Naruto Maru*. The women were told they were going to "Paradise" where there was no malaria. The Army nurses had arrived at the mission with only their uniforms, but thanks to the nuns they each left with three dresses made from sheets, underwear and a blanket plus a few other belongings. Anderson recalled, 'We were loaded onto a truck, taken into Rabaul and onto a boat . . . Imagine our joy and surprise when to greet us were sixty familiar faces. Our officers who had been captured." Talking with the men was forbidden, nonetheless it occurred. Conditions were typical of sea voyages provided by the Japanese for POWs; they reached Yokohama, Japan, on 14 July 1942 exhausted, unwashed and hungry.

Upon arrival the women were separated from the men and taken to the Bund Hotel, much to the surprise of the hotel staff. They were accommodated in a large rat-infested room where they were joined by an elderly American, Mrs Jones, caught in the Aleutian Islands. Marjory Anderson remembered, "We always said it was fortunate we went to the Bund Hotel first because they had gigantic rats there and in three years time we would've eaten those rats! We were all that hungry then." In the dining room was a gleaming array of cutlery but the food did not fulfil expectations! They were allowed to walk in the park and garden and were issued with toothbrushes and powder. Three weeks later they were moved to the Yokohama Amateur Rowing Club on the waterfront. Anderson wrote, "Very happy. Conditions better." There were no bedrooms so the administrative nurses slept in the middle portion of the large room on the second floor and the Methodists and Army nurses were at either end.

The women were initially strictly confined to their room but communications temporarily existed. On the first day at the rowing club the women heard Australian voices below. They eased a hole in the floor and found they could speak to Australian soldiers. They sang to each other in code and the men threw up messages attached to pieces of soap. The soldiers soon left and then their only source of information was the *Nippon Times* (a pro-Japanese newspaper printed in English), which they received until January 1943, and vague gossip from the guards who sometimes translated newspaper articles; as well they followed the maps in the Japanese newspapers if the guards left them about.

They doubted the truthfulness of these Japanese sources.

The Yokohama club was beautifully appointed with full recreational facilities. They were issued with slippers, tooth powder, brushes, soap and long straw mattresses. They had clean lavatories and cold showers were always available and they were occasionally allowed hot baths, particularly if they performed manual work. There were numerous old *Time* magazines which they cut up to decorate their room. They took advantage of ping-pong sets, badminton and cards, and regularly played contract bridge with cards made by Mrs Bignell. During the warmer months they sunbaked and swam in the club's pool, and in the harbour until the coast guards threatened to shoot them. Armistice Day services were held and the Methodist missionary nurses held ecumenical Sunday services (including hymns) which the Japanese generally respected. The Army nurses attended unless the Japanese made it difficult, but not all the administrative nurses did so. Mrs Bignell organized occasional concerts or sing-a-longs, and the women had birthday parties for each other and family or friends, with everyone bringing their own food. Cards made of paper and coloured pencil drawings were gifts. In February 1943 they issued two editions of the *POW*, not comparable to the innovative *Camp Chronicle* of the Sumatran camp.

POW   **1st Edition**   **1.2.43**

Deaths: On Tuesday Jan. 26 at his residence Yokohama "Nippon Times" passed away. It is rumoured that his death was caused by the rapid advance of "Australianosis" which he contracted in the South.

Recipe for Cabbage: By Maisie Mae. Select leaves carefully, do not wash, cut up and simmer for 10 minutes in washing up water in tin dish (preferably rusty) when half cooked place under cold tap for ten minutes, sprinkle with rancid margarine (do not use salt or pepper). Serve as cold as possible. It's sure to be thrown out one way or another.

Holiday Resorts: Lake View Guest House wishes to notify the residents of Yokohama that it is under new management as from February 1. Owing to Australian domestics the prestige of the house has been ruined. It will be under strict Japanese supervision in future. Efficiency guaranteed. We cater for the best.

Edition 2   8.2.43

Meat Recipe: 1½ lbs horse flesh. *Tuesday*: cook for 3 hours. *Wednesday and Thursday*: repeat and for same length of time. *Friday*: cut into pieces and cook again. *Saturday*: put through mincer. Divide in half. Give some to "my friend" and the remainder make into sandwiches for the Shrine. Starving us, where oh where is the Shrine.

There was a limit to the amount people knew and there was nothing to verify or extend their knowledge. The Sumatran camp at least had new learning experiences because of the diversity of the people. Mrs Jones, the American, had a wide general knowledge that enlivened discussions but the others quickly knew each other too well. The *POW* included recipes and the women talked, wrote and dreamed of food and would wake salivating, especially when they were hungrier in Totsuka, their camp in 1944–45. In January 1943 they were issued with cushions, records (which were confiscated after five days) and magazines, and the Red Cross sent them Japanese books. In October 1943 all books were temporarily confiscated. The club's extensive library was used until padlocked, but at night the internees would take out the screws from the door and read secretly. Empire Day was celebrated and the camp ran its own Melbourne Cup. On the Emperor of Japan's birthday in April they had to bow and parade outside in their flimsy garments, although it was very cold.

A week after the women arrived at the club, Japanese lessons commenced. The Japanese had also wanted the women in Sumatra to learn but they refused to do so unless they had paper and pencils and the idea never came to fruition. For the women in Japan the efforts were more systematic but they were neither motivated nor easily able to grasp the language. Most of the guards could speak fragmented English but Parker taught one to sing "God Save the King" which he sang delightedly. Every evening the women were ordered to bow in the direction of the Emperor's palace but they would say "Damn the Emperor! God save the King", and would say the same when they received their monthly supplies. A picture of the King and Queen of Great Britain hung on the wall of the club and because the guards did not know this they allowed the women to bow to that. The Japanese lessons were eventually abandoned but mutual communication was established.

The Chief of Police, who was in charge of them, permitted recreational activities but the internees were employed to make envelopes and silk bags for monetary remuneration. Mrs Bignell wrote:

> The Chiefo has come not to tell us we're pearls,
> but you must abide by the rules.
> As you'll find Japanese people are no fools.
> Look after your health if you want to keep well.
> What we'll do for you we can't just tell.
> You just work at your leisure, not force of course!
> You will get your measure
> See foreign woman we can't understand
> Japanese woman is far beneath man
> But we'll try hard to please you so that your troubles are few.[31]

The work was dull but not strenuous. Thousands of envelopes had to be glued but, despite the fact they were constantly watched, some of the women managed to slip notes in English into the envelopes in the hope of broadening knowledge of their plight. They discovered that the glue when cooked for a lengthy period with a little salt or sugar was palatable and tasted like arrow-root, so they ate rather than glued. Their other task was knitting small silk bags in which the Japanese kept images of their gods. They also realized this task had benefits for themselves. The silk was unravelled and used to make a yarn which they knitted into underwear, cardigans, other pieces of clothing and towels which most did not have. The yarn was made by teasing the cotton wool from their sanitary napkins and rolling it around the silk; most of the women had stopped menstruating but nobody told the Japanese and all but the elderly Mrs Jones received a monthly issue. While in Yokohama they also received monthly soap and sugar and, less regularly, toilet paper. Other physical activities included clearing the area surrounding the club, and during the winter months the women were sent outside to cart ashes when the coal ran out or to collect firewood, tasks which Anderson, at least, quite enjoyed as she was out in the open. Their first pay, eighty-one sen, was issued in September 1942 and thereafter payment was irregular. The Army nurses had no other money. The internees could only buy brushes, tooth powder, wooden clogs and dyes through their female guard, and had no direct contact with local shopkeepers. They could not buy extra food and existed on rations, food they scavenged and Red Cross parcels.

The internees signed "no-escape" forms but any escape was prevented by the fact that they had nowhere to go and were guarded except on a few rare occasions. They were constantly with a female guard whom they jestingly called "Mama San" and one or two male guards. Mama San was formerly the matron of a home for delinquent boys. The male guards slept away from the building, but she slept in the room with the internees, spied on them and told tales to the other guards so the women got into trouble; however she would feign friendliness when Red Cross supplies arrived. Mama San ate her hot meals in front of the internees who existed on a monotonous diet. Their breakfast was normally bread, two tablespoons of the previous day's rice mixed with water, the same quantity of soya bean soup, and a cup of water or green tea. Lunch was a small cup of dry rice with hot water or green tea and at night a small cup of rice and half a cup of stew. The stew consisted of questionable bits of meat (removed before serving), the outside leaves of cauliflower, cabbage, carrot tops, seaweed and sometimes salt. If there was no salt they used sea water to cook their food. Occasionally fish soup, seaweed soup, small lettuce leaves, bad or dried fish or rhubarb were issued but fruit (apart from some mandarins or plums) was generally not available. Potatoes were issued for a time and one or two slices of sour bread were supplied each day. It was sometimes fresh but mostly stale and mildewed; they ate it anyway as the chewing motion when eating the furred bread made them feel less hungry. Sometimes they chewed toilet paper and later grasses for the same effect. They became adept at collecting seaweed, refuse and rotten vegetables from the environs of the rowing club grounds and later boiled rusty nails to add nutrients to the water. They normally took it in turns to steal whenever possible from the guards. The thief would take the food to her group of friends, either Army, administrative or Methodist.

Two Japanese cooked for the internees but in 1943 the Japanese became more organized and three internees assisted the cooks as part of their chores.

Rations improved temporarily at the beginning of 1943 and in April Anderson recorded fifteen consecutive days of meat at least once a day. This gradually decreased in accordance with the comments of the new supervisor who claimed that the police were poor, therefore the internees should be reduced to Japanese food. In the spring and summer months the women did more outdoor work and were told to dig gardens although they were given nothing to plant. They stole

Daily Schedule Effective from 1.2.43

No.	Time	Particulars	Remarks
1	6.55	Rising Signal	Whistle shall be blown by Official
2	7.00	Roll Call	Roll call after rising
3	7.10	Toilet	
4	7.35	Room Cleaning	
5	8.00	Breakfast	
6	8.30	Recess	Should have fresh air in the outdoors on fine day
7	9.00	Works	
8	11.00	Free	Should be spent for washing etc. or basking if fine
9	12.00 M.D.	Tiffin	
10	12.30 p.m.	Recess	Can be out to [sic] the ground on fine day
11	1.30	Works	
12	2.45	Tea Time	
13	3.15-4.00	Works	
14	4.10	Room Cleaning	
15	5.00	Supper	After supper not allowed to be out
16	5.30-8.00	Free	About ½ hour should be kept for Japanese language lessons and rest for taking bath or cleaning body with warm water
17	8.00	Roll Call	
18	8.30	Retire	

N.B.

A. Each period shall be notified with whistle by the Official.

B. Working hours must be strictly and earnestly kept.

C. Schedule must be strictly carried on except on special occasions.

D. On shopping orders, names of articles, quantity and names of buyers must be clearly described in English and handed to the Official.

E. A medical examination should be executed on a certain Wednesday of each month.

F. During the recess any body who wishes to be out to the ground [sic] must get permission of the Official.

Anyone who violates the above shall be severely punished.

By Order

Chief of the Kagacho Police Station
Y. Nakanishi

seeds from the kitchen, but at times they were confined inside for weeks and so could not tend the plots; if anything ripened the guards invariably ate it.

The eighth day of each month was Degradation or Humiliation Day, when the vegetables that were issued were thrown into a cesspit. After the internees had retrieved the vegetables they had to kneel and bow in the direction of the Emperor's palace before they were allowed to cook them. Humiliation Day sometimes took the form of eating scraps in a pig bucket. The women normally ate with Western cutlery and used jam tins as plates. Visitors arrived to view the internees and ate good food. "We had to bow to them. They would ask were we happy because we were in Japan, and we told them no, it was because we were Australians."[32] Anderson wrote in 1943 that the Chief of Police and other officials told the internees they were enjoying a "vacation by the sea", but the cold of the winter months and the cool weather for most of the year was one of the most trying difficulties they faced.

The winter months created a fervour of activity amongst the women in order to become as warm as possible. Mrs Jones had large trunks of clothing which she shared but she was very small and her clothes were of no use to the Army nurses who were mostly tall and had bigger builds. The Methodists brought clothing, underwear and sheets from Rabaul, as they had had time to collect their belongings, but they shared amongst themselves and only lent a few remaining items. The Army and administrative nurses, who had only been able to collect a few belongings, and Mrs Bignell, who had nothing at all, made their sheet dresses from Rabaul warmer by padding them with cotton wool; they also used canvas from the sentry box for dresses. Four yards of thick woollen material were given to each internee in October 1942, out of which they made trousers with a sewing machine lent to them by the Japanese for three weeks. When the trousers wore out they wore them back to front. Just before Christmas 1942 they were also given a towel and badly made woollen underwear which they dyed.

Their bed coverings were poor quality eiderdowns made from cotton wool and scraps of material; they were given as many as three, but they were heavy not warm so the internees slept in pairs for warmth. Two mattresses were put together, one eiderdown underneath and the others on top with their blankets from Rabaul, and still they were cold. Hot water bottles were issued, and they used to crowd around a heater/stove that was installed in the dining room. There was insufficient firewood or coal so they removed the palings from the fence and carried in ashes. The women would sit closely together in their three groups and rub each other's extremities, a task which became more vital when the heater was taken away in April 1943 and not returned.

The internees received a measure of overseas relief during their three years in Japan. During their internment they were given twelve individual parcels each and one bulk package which they eked out. The parcels contained food, sometimes clothing and flimsy shoes or toiletries. The first parcels were delivered on 24 December 1942, by an official of the Red Cross, Delegate Pestalozzi. The issue contained: two bags sugar (a hundred pounds each), one carton soap, four cartons Maybella, five cases fruit (twenty-five pounds), two cases meat, and twenty-five pounds cocoa; and each person received a parcel containing one pound chocolate, condensed milk, twenty ounces cheese, sugar, live pate, apple pudding, golden syrup, creamed rice, tomatoes, biscuits, margarine, beefsteak pudding, tea and bacon. He returned on 7 January 1943 but the women were bitter that he did not come again to answer their questions or do anything further for them. Unbeknown to the internees the IRCC did make further applications to visit but these were rejected.[33] The Army nurses' names were not transmitted to Australia.

Christmas was celebrated with some splendour. The room was decorated with pictures from magazines and a Christmas tree, and they made cards and gifts for each other and remembered relatives and friends in Australia. The Commanding Officer of the guards objected to the decorations and only the tree was allowed to remain. They placed a horseshoe on the door which was also removed as the guard said it was suggestive of a "V for victory". Christmas Eve dinner consisted of steak, vegetables and cakes. Christmas Day was "dull, bridge most of the day" but Mr Ball, the civilian in charge of the internees, and his young son visited briefly that evening when they had community singing around the fire. A "crazy whist party" organized by Joyce Oldroyd-Harris, an administrative nurse, was held on New Year's Eve.

The women had minimal freedom of movement and hoped only for their return to Australia. In April a ten-foot wall was built, reducing the size of the grounds so they had very little space to walk and could see nothing when on ground level. They tried to speak to the workmen to get news but, as with the information given by the guards, they did not believe the little they were told. The hope of being repatriated was always strong but particularly in the first year and a half. Keast, now Mrs McPherson, said:

> When first we went there they really thought we might've been exchanged and they had what they called the White Cross ships in the harbour. One of the cooks used to tell us a bit and he said we were going to be exchanged but the last ship went and that's when they put the boot in. We weren't being exchanged, we were all prisoners, and that's when they cut the food down too.

The guards told them who had been repatriated on the ships and where they had gone; for instance, on 13 September 1943 they were told that women and children had left for America. The Australian government did not know where they were and was unable to arrange exchange despite negotiations with the Japanese government. A list of the names of civilians who were in New Britain and were believed to be prisoners of the Japanese was forwarded to the United Kingdom for submission to the Japanese government in the event of an exchange being possible.

As with the official visits to the nurses' camps in Sumatra, no benefit accrued to the internees. In February 1943 forms were filled out for the Army stating personal particulars but nothing eventuated. Parker attempted to broach the subject of the internees' return to Australia with the Chief of Police and a Foreign Office official but the police censored the queries and they were ignored. Anderson wrote on 4 March 1943, "Visit by San Francisco [new Chief] in pm. Stony answers to questions. Quite convinced people do not know of our whereabouts." Parker tried again around April to extract this information from an interpreter but he also ignored her. An official military visitor inspected their food but the cook showed him the guards' issue and hid the internees' stew. In September 1943 they were promised an audience with an official from Tokyo who arrived with ten others but the audience did not transpire. They were left with their guards who could only affect their daily treatment.

There was always a degree of uncertainty about their future. None of the groups (Army, administrative or Methodist) could hide within the larger group, as the nurses in Sumatra could, because there were only nineteen people. Everything they did was scrutinized unless they were devious. The guards alternated between police guards and naval personnel, all with different but increasingly cruel personalities. The police guards predominated and the women considered they were "rejects" from the forces because a number were very ill. The internees partly explained the irrational behaviour of these guards as due to ill-health. All the women except Callaghan ate the remains from the guards' plates even if they had tuberculosis like the guard "Cougher".

Each morning and evening through captivity *bungo* (the equivalent to *tenko*) was held. Infrequently they were lined up at gunpoint but more often the punishment was face slapping. The women customarily removed their glasses and dentures before *bungo* but some of these were confiscated and not returned. One guard knocked out the glass and wore the frames. During the early months of 1943 the guards lectured them on manners, but at least one face was slapped every night and the internees were forced to say they were hot when they were freezing in front of the warmly clad guard. The guards that replaced these were not as physically cruel but cut rations and laughed when the women complained. On other occasions hot water was stopped or some of their pleasures taken away as punishment, but during the last two years a hit without provocation was common. During the last part of 1943 and early 1944 a guard they called "Basher", who also had tuberculosis, was employed, and Anderson wrote ambiguously in her diary on 8 February 1944, "Dance of swords 1800 hours, battle begins in earnest". The three women on kitchen chores had been given a brazier full of coals by the cook — a welcome present as they had no fire, no hot food and were depressed. Basher was furious that they had not asked his permission because the cook had a lower position than his. He dragged out those who were in bed (it was 6.00 p.m. but very cold) and gave them all lectures and deportment lessons (they had to bow to the knee when they served him food), lunged at them with swords, bashed Parker and continued to be cruel. His duties quickly ceased and the pleasant relief guard "Kusnatz" stayed with them, but died shortly afterwards. Other guards such as "Happy San" and "Popper San" were very kind. Sometimes the women could hardly stop themselves from laughing when the small Japanese tried to hit them — on one occasion a guard had to stand on a box to smack Parker's face.

It became a point of principle amongst the group that the Japanese they hated would never see them cry, but they did so privately. Anderson recalled, "To keep us humiliated and busy was the object of our captors. They failed in the former and had an overwhelming victory in the latter. No matter what we were asked to do we appeared to do it willingly." Even the Humiliation Days did not curb the certainty that they as Australians were superior. The nurses said, "The Japs did not understand why we were so cheerful."

Sister Kay Parker was appointed spokeswoman by the Japanese and she had a natural bearing appropriate for the role. She was a tall, very articulate woman and could reason them out of most situations. Anderson said, "Kay, she was just tremendous. We all owe our lives to Kay many times . . . She was just that sort of person. She was a born leader . . . she had the courage. She would never let them see that they had intimidated her in any way whatsoever." The Japanese directed most of their inquiries through her, especially in the final year when they were less cruel and realized the women would not escape, but as leader she was occasionally slapped as an example to the others. She engendered a positive attitude and was an unceasing worker, giving out the Red Cross issues and making work rosters for the whole group. She had to be scrupulously fair in distribution of supplies, as did the three cook-girls; favouritism was not permitted. Whereas no one leader emerged amongst the Army nurses in Sumatra, perhaps because they had an overall camp commander, Parker emerged as leader of these Army nurses for whom, as their Senior Sister, she assumed particular responsibility. Parker could not solve all problems and Mrs Jones was a valuable peacemaker and adviser when the different personalities and interests of the Army, administrative and Methodist personnel were at variance.

The spirit and defiance of these women frightened the Japanese, who temporarily changed the internees' accommodation on 19 August 1943 after the internees suggested they would kidnap the Emperor and tell him their story when he came to Yokohama to review the Sea Scouts. The internees hoped when they were moved that they were going onto the White Cross ship then in dock. Instead for twelve days they were taken to the police station from which they saw their first tram since leaving Australia. Their quarters were comfortable, they were able to have a warm bath once a week, and the food was much better; they returned to the Yokohama rowing club with the blackout curtains which they later made into underwear. The supervision at the police station was relaxed and everyone was very kind; they even kept watch for the guard, "Happy", while he slept. However, when they returned to their previous residence they found their gardens had been destroyed.

"More Better She Die"

During their years of internment in Japan the nurses were not asked by the Japanese to use their professional skills, but they did look after each other. The extreme cold and their progressively poor diet resulted in loss of weight and deterioration in health. A dentist visited in late 1943 and again before they were moved from the Yokohama club in July 1944. Some of the internees cut their hair or shaved it off to keep clean. Most had repeated attacks of malaria although in Yokohama they were issued with mosquito nets. Apart from minor colds, flu and bronchitis, their main complaints were weakness and deficiency diseases such as beri-beri that were most obvious in the final year of captivity. During the first two years in Japan a doctor visited every two to three months but nearly always pronounced them fit; if not, he only occasionally issued quinine or gave an injection and more often prescribed aspirin for every illness. One of the Methodists had a small supply of quinine which she shared amongst her friends. Parker suffered intense abdominal pain in September 1943 and Callaghan and Cullen accompanied her to the maternity hospital where she was admitted. The conditions were so unhygienic she preferred to die amongst friends, and returned as quickly as she could. She later recovered. After they had left the rowing club the doctor came less often and gave no treatment to Callaghan who had contracted tuberculosis. The Japanese maintained "more better she die".

The freezing cold of the winter months of 1944 affected the attitude and desires of the internees more than the lack of food, privacy or news — they desperately and foremost wanted warmth. Keast reports that "It is worse to be cold than to be hungry", and Anderson says that now she is not afraid of hunger, but still fears the cold. The ice froze their few clothes on the washing-line and ice formed in their buckets of water. Unlike the previous year, they had no stove and only their hot water bottles which by March were only permitted at night. Sometimes they were allowed to stay in bed all day to keep warm. Coal arrived but was not for their personal use and their hands froze using the cold glue. The food never improved enough to warm them and they were too weak to exercise very much.

Despite their weakened state, Christmas celebrations were more innovative. An undertaker arrived with Red Cross Christmas parcels of western foods, some of which were bad. The Japanese did show respect for the aged and young, as the women in Sumatra also noted; that did not necessarily mean rations were affected. Sometimes however, Mama San gave Mrs Jones a treat and at Christmas it was a piece of apple. Grace Kruger, an administrative nurse, held a New Year's Eve party and New Year's Day was heralded with a full meal and a party given by Joyce Oldroyd-Harris.

Friendships which had been established in pre-war days strengthened but the Methodists and Oldroyd-Harris were more friendly with the Army nurses. Oldroyd-Harris had not known the administrative nurses well as she had only arrived in Rabaul on 22 December 1941. The women as a group had to relate to each other as they were in such close contact but personal dislikes still existed. It was within the smaller groupings that relations were content.

On 13 April 1944 McLellan, an administrative nurse, wrote in her diary: "News of new house. Good news of female staff not coming."[34] It was with a certain amount of hope that they packed their few belongings and left the rowing club on 9 July 1944. McLellan wrote in her diary, "All very busy packing — oh the tins and rubbish all so precious." The building was stripped.

They were taken thirty miles away to a farmhouse, formerly a tuberculosis hospital, set in pretty surroundings at Totsuka. It was close to a chestnut grove, to which one amenable guard, "Popper San", escorted them to pick the nuts in the early morning, and had a view of snow-capped Mount Fuji. Anderson wrote in her diary: "New home nice and comfortable. Most happy in new surroundings." The house was light and airy and accommodation was better as four slept to a room. The friendships and divisions that had previously formed were reflected in the sleeping arrangements. Callaghan, Cullen, Parker and Whyte slept in one room, Anderson, Keast (these two were great friends),

Mrs Jones and Oldroyd-Harris in a second room, the four Methodist missionaries in another and the administrative nurses and Mrs Bignell in the remainder. As there was no heating the women spent as much time in bed as possible to keep warm. Callaghan woke each morning after a feverish night with ice on her forehead. The lavatories were pits that the internees sometimes emptied onto the garden, thus creating a continuous odour, but mostly the local gardener took the sewerage for his own garden. There were no showers, only one pump that they worked manually and no hot water except from the kitchen. The guards would allow them a bucket of hot water to unfreeze the pump in the morning. They filled buckets of water in the evening which froze over during the night but most of the women would break the ice every day and wash — if they had stopped they would not have been able to resume. When the guards were not looking they stole hot water from the kitchen for washing and also took water from the Japanese communal baths which they filled and lit. The internees had two proper baths in the year. They still retained their modesty and would not bathe when the guards were present.

The women worked much harder than previously at manual chores. Parker organized daily rosters that combined Army, administrative and Methodist personnel, but she would always go herself if the women were too sick or she thought support was required. At the same time as their colleagues in Sumatra were working to produce food these women were also digging and planting gardens, but the gardens in Japan were more successful. They still worked in the kitchen —

sometimes carrying up to a hundred buckets a day from the pump to the kitchen three hundred yards away — cleaned the house, chopped trees and wood and carted coal. In sunny weather they would work slowly. Sometimes they worked in the fields nearby where they were able to pilfer vegetables. They no longer received payment or regular issues of sugar, soap and sanitary napkins; instead they were issued with a small quantity of cotton wool and told to use leaves for toilet paper. Occasionally extra food was issued as a reward for work.

The internees dug air-raid trenches for the Japanese but were not allowed to use them themselves, and in the winter months they were forced to shovel paths in the snow for the warmly dressed Japanese. The Army nurses no longer had any shoes. They went barefoot or in socks (they were given two pairs), and either wrapped a few rags around a plank of wood to their feet or wore Japanese clogs. Their hands were bare unless they wrapped rags around them. As they grew progressively weaker these chores became more difficult, but the Japanese were often inconsistent and did not always demand physical work or that a task be finished. If a person fell over, the others continued but the sick could rest.

By early January 1945 most of the women weighed around six stone and each group looked after its own. Callaghan was bedridden and Parker insisted on undertaking her nursing as much as possible so the others were protected from the infection. Staff Nurse Keast insisted, "We knew we were going home and weren't going to leave our bones there. But we couldn't

126

have lived another winter, we hadn't a hope. Some of the girls weren't walking around, you had to help them." Anderson could not walk up two steps by the end of her captivity.

Some of the Japanese who lived nearby secretly placed fruit or vegetables on their stairs. Moreover, the internees bargained with the Red Cross issues. On Christmas Day 1944 they received five Red Cross parcels which they frugally kept in reserve. With the cigarettes from these parcels and other goods they bribed a Japanese woman ("Mum") who lived in a shack behind the main farmhouse to cook them sweet potatoes when the guards were not about. These varied in quantity and quality but Mum's price for cooking a small amount escalated and she did not always meet her commitments. In late 1945 McLellan noted in her diary the transactions she had with "Mum":

Pair Shoes — Mine	Bag sweet potatoes (80 lbs), bag peanuts (8 lbs)
Pair Shoes — Bowie's	Bottle soya sauce (6 pints), meso (3 lbs)
6 cakes soap	18 eggs
Wooden Red Cross Box	soya sauce (3 pints)
8 cakes soap	soya beans (32 lbs)
2 tins boot polish + 2 cakes soap	Potatoes (16 lbs)
1 pr. Ghettas (children's)	Roasted beans (1 lb)
1 pr. Ghettas (children's)	Cooked rice — 1 plate for 5 days + 6 potatoes
Jar face cream	3 eggs
Red Cross Boxes (cardboard)	Milk tins (1 lb), sundry plates rice, flour, fat, meso, soya, leeks, diakon, turnips, etc.

Pair pants	plate cooked rice for one week
2 tins boot polish	potatoes and onions (16 lbs)
+ 2 cakes soap	
Yellow shirt	plate cooked rice for one week
1 packet tobacco	16 lbs potatoes
1 packet tobacco	8 lbs soya beans
+ 1 cake soap	

Bowie was A.M. Bowman, an administrative nurse, *meso* was bean curd, *Ghettas* were wooden clogs and *diakon* was chaff.

These transactions were done in secret and food shared within the particular groups. There were numerous stray dogs around the camp and when the internees received meat in their stew they did not question its appearance — dogs' and cats' entrails and watery rice. The women continued to take turns stealing from the guards, which was easier to do than in Yokohama, and muttered abuse at the guards when they served them their hot food. By 1945 they mostly saved their daily rations for one meal a day in the evening; usually watery rice with carrot and turnip tops served with tea. Even though they ate before they went to bed some of the women would walk about at night unable to sleep for hunger.

The internees lived day by day, never allowing themselves to lose faith but supporting and bolstering each other when they were depressed. Anderson stated, "If we had given up we wouldn't have come back, it's as simple as that. If we gave up hope we'd have just died." Mrs Jones was a great comfort as she was old but managed so well. Manners were still retained and Mrs Jones and Mrs Bignell, like Mrs Hinch in Sumatra, were never called by their Christian names. Christmas 1944 was a sad occasion, despite Red Cross supplies and a present of potatoes from "Mum". The bitter cold, sickness and lack of communication made a sense of purpose very difficult to maintain, although from the wartime activities they saw around them and the news from the guards they concluded that Japan was losing the war.

During the three years the women were in Japan they did not hear from their relatives nor were they allowed to write to them. However, in the last year they could see that the war was going badly for Japan and their spirits rose accordingly. They saw bombing and fires in the distance and would count the planes that left Atsugi aerodrome nearby but would cheer for the Allies. They told the Japanese if they were good they would not be hit. They read bits from the guards' newspapers and heard news of President Roosevelt's death in April which made the guards deliriously happy, and of the devastating bombing raids on Tokyo and Yokohama. In June pamphlets were dropped which told of a threatened invasion and in July they knew about Mr Curtin's death.

The Japanese defeats raised the hopes of the internees but had the opposite effect on the Japanese who became suspicious and envious. In February 1945 the group was accused of contacting Allied airmen and threatened with a sword. The house of one of their guards was destroyed and the guards, who were also hungry, raided the internees' Red Cross supplies and burnt what they left. No bread was issued for two weeks and they were told to prepare to die. On 3 July 1945, however, they were visited by an official Red Cross representative who told them nobody knew where they were and that the European war was over. McLellan wrote in her diary on 3 July 1945:

> . . . information gleaned etc. as to how we have and should have been treated shows more and more the vileness of the people. What we should be getting as POWs:
>
> Y [yen] 50 monthly to draw on.
> ¾ lb rice ration daily plus-
> Baths and toilet appliances (?)
> Letters and cables home monthly
> No manual labour or abuse
> Warm clothing and bedding. Heating.
>
> What we got:
> Watery rice and green stodge
> Woodcutting and trench digging
> One futon [quilt], no heating, cotton shirt,
> "us" [warmth of each other?] in midwinter
> A "clout" often without provocation
>
> . . . All I can say is Heaven help those
> in a large camp. Poor men! Unless they have a Mum
> who has been our Salvation . . .

The Red Cross representative obtained permission to send their names to Australia but it was not until 8 August 1945 that 2nd Echelon Army Headquarters were told that the Army nurses were POWs interned at Totsuka and in "good health". Parker had been informed late in July, by a Red Cross letter, that the information had been forwarded to Switzerland. In August they were allowed to write a carefully worded letter home.

Staff Nurse D.C. Keast to Keast family, 11 August 1945

Darling . . .

Swiss Red Cross first visit July. Cable despatched. First letter.
Anxious to hear from you. Am very well. Mother, Dad don't
worry. Nineteen in nice country house very comfortable,
beautiful surroundings, airy bedroom with Andy. We six well.
No work except clean house. Voluntary gardening, library,
held three years in Japan. Celebrate birthdays . . . [personal
details].

Looking forward to early return to you. Food, clothing,
medical supplies, periodically from Red Cross, gratefully appreciated!

. . . Tootie

This together with the fact that the Emperor made a
radio broadcast for the first time and there was no
midday alert on 15 August 1945 cheered the women
considerably.

On 17 August 1945 the internees were told that
peace had been declared that day. Jean McLellan, now
Mrs Harwood, recalled:

One morning one of our guards or officers, a funny little old
man who said he couldn't speak a word of English, could never
understand us if we asked for anything, came round to where
we all were and just out of the blue wanted to shake hands with
us all. "The war is finished peace is here", and then he sang the
hymn "Jesus loves me this I know". He sang that in English. He
could speak quite good English. That's how we knew the war
was over.

The women were free but warned to remain within
the boundaries of the compound and as they were
afraid of reprisals this advice was followed. Food suddenly improved and they were given half a side of raw

beef and control of the food supply. The nurses ate huge quantities regardless of the medical hazards they knew existed when gluttony followed prolonged starvation. Their stomachs swelled and they were sick but they continued to eat. The guards gave them twenty tins of salmon each, two bottles of beer, a pound of butter and a tin of milk. The guards were attentive and pleaded with them to tell the Americans they were good as otherwise they were sure they would be killed. The Japanese gave them a coat each because the Army nurses' uniforms were in tatters. A doctor arrived and they were given medicine. A white cross made from sheets was placed outside and food parcels, far more than they required, were dropped. They were fed and warmer, but were still in a foreign land. Their guards were doubled and they were, as always, afraid of retaliation.

Captivity was monotonous but at least in Sumatra the women had greater opportunities to use their experiences and to learn from a variety of people. The life in Japan lacked this multicultural diversity and these women were not as imaginative, partly because they were issued with more comforts and did not have to make their own recreation. Friendships strengthened in adversity, but despite the close contact their original groupings remained. Eileen Callaghan only wanted to survive to die in Australia, an attitude they all adopted. They were reduced to hunger and complete poverty but they did not have to live with constant death or total destitution.

Release

Three years and seven months of imprisonment removed the Australian Army nurses interned in Japan and Sumatra from the events of the outside world. Detailed plans for the recovery of POWs from Japanese camps — covering a vast area in the Pacific that included Borneo, Sumatra, Burma, Korea and Japan — were organized well before the end of the war, but very little was known of the Australian Army nurses. The declaration of peace activated the plans to repatriate some 14,340 Australian prisoners, the survivors of an original 22,400 who had been captured by the Japanese, mainly in February 1942 on Singapore Island. By chance, and despite obstacles placed by the Japanese, the camps at Totsuka and Loebok Linggau were found. The nurses in Japan were rescued in late August and were among the first group of British Commonwealth repatriates to reach Australian reception groups in Manila on 3 September 1945. It was not until 16 September that the other nurses in Sumatra were discovered. Liberated in poor physical and mental condition after nearly four years of uncertainty and no news, they were given an overwhelming reception. Physical and emotional readjustment had to take place without the support of the friends who had constantly been with them during the ordeal.

The lack of information regarding the whereabouts and condition of Australian POWs in Japanese hands was initially a cause of great dissatisfaction to the general public, who did not understand the difficulties involved and consequently criticized the government, the Red Cross, the Protecting Power (Switzerland), and various other charitable and aid organizations. Although the Japanese agreed to apply the Convention on Treatment of Prisoners of War (27 July 1929) *mutatis mutandis* there was no way of compelling Japanese fulfilment of obligations. Large distances were involved, the Allies were unable to get regular relief to POWs or establish mail routes, and there were differences in living standards and attitudes. Dr J. Newman Morris, in an Australian Red Cross address in 1944, said, "The Japanese will never give a reply to a question, and the camps vary greatly according to the character of the individual Japanese man in authority."[35] The Allied nations could only make repeated requests for cooperation through direct representations and via the IRCC and the Protecting Power.

The almost complete failure of the Japanese to supply information regarding personnel held captive, or who had died during captivity, necessitated the 2nd Echelon Group of the Adjutant General's Branch (the base records organization) coordinating methods of extracting as much information from available sources as possible. The Censorship authorities extracted particulars such as names, prison camp addresses, dates and other prisoners named, from mail. The Department of Information recorded prisoner radio messages, some of which were genuine, broadcast by the Japanese. Officers of the 2nd Echelon organization also assisted in the instruction of contact and interrogating officers, and compiled information received. Amongst their numerous activities 2nd Echelon also constructed lexicographical rolls of AMF personnel and their known particulars. After the broadcast messages in March 1943, the women in Sumatra were reported POWs in a Sumatran camp (Palembang) in October, November and December 1943. At least one request was made on 20 October 1943 to the Protecting Power inquiring as to the whereabouts, health and nature of employment of the nurses in Sumatra; this was not answered although in December 1943 the cablegram was acknowledged and the IRCC reported that Ada Syer was interned in Sumatra.[36]

In November 1944 the POWs Information Bureau, which amongst other activities prepared details used in a message service to POWs in the Far East, received an interrogation report of seventy-eight AIF POWs rescued when the *Rokyu Maru*, an unmarked Japanese transport carrying Australian and British personnel from Singapore to Japan, was sunk. It had been attacked and sunk by American submarines on 12 September 1944. The report stated that one survivor saw a list of fourteen Australian nurses said to be in a camp at Palembang, Sumatra, in August 1944 and twenty-four nurses who were killed and another twenty-two who were missing. Other survivors also saw the list but reported the number at Palembang as twenty-two and understood they were living with the civilian white women. This information was not placed on the 2nd Echelon files.[37] In September 1945, Colonel A.M. Sage (Matron-in-Chief AMF), told Flight Sister Beryl Chandler, a member of No. 2 Medical Air Evacuation Transport unit (MAETU) and part of the team which rescued the nurses in Sumatra, that Army authorities in Melbourne had heard rumours of the Banka Island massacre but refused to believe such a tragedy.[38] The 2nd Echelon Personal Files reported the six Army nurses in Japan were "missing" or "missing believed POW" in May 1942 and all were reported POWs on 8 August 1945. No further information appears to have reached Australia concerning their whereabouts.

The nineteen internees in Japan were in the midst of the American occupation of Japan when they were found in late August. A female IRCC delegate and an English-speaking Japanese man visited the Totsuka camp on 23 August 1945 and McLellan noted, ". . . very astounded at all that pertains to us — cannot understand this that and the other". Each inmate was given medicine, a dress, and a pair of shoes, and a list of their names was sent to Geneva. "General health of party is fair, rapidly improving since recent increase in rations, with the exception of: Eileen Callaghan aged 32 years who is suffering from advanced bilateral tuberculosis aggravated by lack of medical care."[39] A joint message from the internees indicated they were all well and would be home soon and an individual message from Eileen Callaghan stated that she was "not very well, do not worry".[40]

American B29s flew over many POW camps including the nurses' camp parachuting supplies to POWs, but making ground contact was more difficult because many of the camp locations were unknown and the behaviour of the defeated Japanese could not always be predicted. The internees made a practice of going down the road near their camp in small groups or singly to look out for occupation forces. On 30 August Lorna Whyte and Jean McLellan went to the village and shouted and waved to an American convoy passing by. On 31 August Whyte and McLellan ran out to collect some air drops and afterwards decided to stay and look at passing vehicles. They saw a jeep containing an American officer and an enlisted man and managed to stop it. The Japanese tried to prevent them from communicating but they made their plight known and the Americans took control. They were told later that another American had seen them in the fields, but he had been informed that they were English women married to Japanese.[41]

Kay Parker immediately saw to it that Eileen Callaghan was attended to and sent home on the first available hospital ship, as she was not physically able to withstand a flight. She was taken on board the American *Marigold* in Yokohama harbour, and later returned on the hospital ship *Tjitjalengka*, reaching Sydney on 12 October 1945, a month after the first of her companions arrived in Australia. The other five Army nurses and the civilians left the camp on 1 September 1945 and spent the night at the Atsugi Aerodrome where they met male POWs. McLellan noted in her diary, "How marvellous has been our treatment after what some of them have been through." They were flown to Okinawa Island where Marjory Anderson, who was five feet eight inches tall and weighed just under six stone, collapsed and was hospitalized with weakness and a severe attack of malaria. She remained there for eight days but the others were flown on to Manila early next morning and were cared for by the Americans. Anderson arrived in Manila the day the others left for Australia.

> . . . Nobody knew when I was coming home and nobody knew where I was . . . It must have been dreadful for the other girls because all my people were waiting when they arrived and all they could tell them was that they had left me on Okinawa Island. What had happened to me after that nobody knew . . . I missed out on all the fun of coming home together with my friends . . . I was wild when I got to the Philippines and found that they had gone out the morning of that afternoon. I'd just missed them by that much.

In Manila she was transferred from the Americans to the Australians and for another eight days enjoyed good food, a new wardrobe and Australian company. A Liberator bomber brought her and a group of servicemen back to Australia. Instead of the usual group of relatives she was met by Sister A.G. Greenwood from Victoria Barracks, Sydney. Greenwood was sent to the aerodrome because Anderson's relatives had persistently endeavoured to find out what had happened to her and there was a chance that the unnamed woman who was returning on 21 September 1945 was Anderson. The nurses had always planned to arrive back in Australia in their uniforms, but in the end only Parker arrived in the salvaged remains of hers in Manila.

The Australian Army was well prepared for the re-

ception of POWs from the Far East. They established
the 2nd Australian POW Reception Group in Singapore
and the 3rd Australian POW Reception Group in
Manila where it acted as a subsidiary force to the
American organization. The bulk of the medical work
in the Philippines was done by the Americans and in
strict accordance with methods of procedure established by the United States Army; the Australian contact teams were only attached to assist with specific
problems applicable to their own and British nationals.
Consequently, the Australian Army nurses and the
civilians were received by the United States Army
Women's Replacement and Disposition Centre. They
were medically examined, accommodated and process-
ed by the Americans in consultation with the 3rd
Australian POW Reception Group, whereas the nurses
in Sumatra were totally cared for by Australians.

The Americans feted and fed the Australians. Keast
recalled, "The Americans killed us with food". When
they finally arrived at Concord Hospital in Sydney the
staff were astounded that they could have abused their
bodies with the quantities of food they had consumed.
Parker had lost nearly seven stone but most of the
larger women had lost from three to five stone. By
the time they left for Australia the Army nurses
weighed between eight and a half and ten and a half
stone. While in Manila they were visited by General
Sir Thomas Blamey, Commander-in-Chief Land
Forces South-West Pacific Area (SWPA) and
Commander-in-Chief AMF, and Colonel Sage sent a
message. The internees saw their first movie in four
years — *Earl Carroll's Vanities* — which produced

astonished gasps as glamorous women, clothes and new hairstyles paraded before them. The women enplaned for Darwin on 12 September 1945 and had an exhausting trip despite the many comforts provided by the Red Cross. Parker undertook her last task as leader of this small group of women (she was appointed Draft Conducting Officer for the duration of the trip to Australia). They arrived in Darwin nervy, weak and unable to cope with the prospect of a proposed immediate connecting flight to Sydney. The Army nurses were given a party whilst the civilian ex-internees watched. The civilians had to seek help for themselves, but the Army nurses were treated at Concord Hospital, where they received, among other things, cosmetics, rugs, underclothes and nightwear.

The rescue of the nurses in Sumatra occurred on 16 September 1945. That it was not later was largely due to the efforts of Haydon Lennard — Senior War Correspondent for the Australian Broadcasting Commission (ABC) and the British Broadcasting Commission (BBC) in New Guinea, China, India, Burma and Pacific theatres — and the flight crew who agreed to assist him. Lennard was interested in the fate of the Australian nurses on the *Vyner Brooke* throughout the war and had been given a letter before he left Australia by Mr and Mrs Trotter for their daughter if he found her. Flight Sister Beryl Chandler of No. 2 MAETU, who had trained at the Brisbane General Hospital with some of the Army nurses, recalled: "Naturally all Australia was shocked at nurses being taken and kept prisoner and their whereabouts concerned us all, civilian and service personnel alike. We fully expected in the early stages of the war that they would be repatriated but as we so sadly know it was not to be."[42] Lennard heard of the Banka Island massacre from inmates of Changi gaol, including Captain A. Curlewis and Major W.A. Tebbutt, formerly a Sydney solicitor, who had assisted Matron Paschke organize the nurses on the *Vyner Brooke*. He had swum ashore and later heard of the massacre. He had also heard that Bullwinkel was the sole survivor, but the subject was kept a close secret by the men as with the women in case of Japanese reprisals. Another inmate reported that Bullwinkel had been seen "going down the river from Palembang, Sumatra, with a small group of nurses some two years ago". Although the internees did not travel by boat during 1943 it would appear they were sighted in their uniforms (as they had hoped they would be) on one of their camp changes.

Lennard was surprised that they were alive as he had attended Chief of Staff Conferences in Ceylon at the invitation of Admiral Lord Louis Mountbatten while the impending invasion of Malaya was planned, and no mention had been made of the possibility that any nurses could be alive. Mountbatten warned General Blamey in June 1945 that impending operations in Malaya might result in the release of large numbers of POWs, including Australians. A.E. Dunstan and other correspondents who interviewed inmates of Changi also heard Bullwinkel's story, but Lennard and Dunstan decided to try and get them out of Sumatra. Lennard obtained a blanket censorship on the story from

Mountbatten's headquarters; Mountbatten was personally interested and approved of the proposal to ask the RAAF to fly into Sumatra to find the nurses. The blanket censorship was hardly needed, for when Lennard addressed some one hundred war correspondents in Singapore's Cathay Building the night before they left on their search, nobody objected to the need to protect the nurses.

On 14 September 1945 the two war correspondents approached Squadron Leader F.W. Madsen, a member of 36 Squadron RAAF based in Singapore for the specific purpose of bringing out POWs from outlying areas, who agreed to pilot the plane. Madsen agreed to take only one war correspondent, Lennard, on board as information on the serviceability of the Palembang airstrip indicated that it was only suitable for light aircraft. Six passengers apart from the normal crew of three were authorized, but a man whose wife was a civilian internee in the camp stowed aboard. Chandler normally flew without a doctor, but the seriousness of the mission induced her to accept the services of Major H.M. Windsor of the 2/14th AGH and his medical orderly Private Prott. Lieutenant-Colonel Hayes of the Royal Army Medical Corps and Major Clough of the Repatriation of Allied Prisoners of War and Internees Organization were the other passengers. The plane left on 15 September 1945 and effected a successful landing at Palembang, where members of the Japanese airforce flagged the plane and senior Japanese officers met it.

Communication difficulties hindered the search efforts as none of the apparently friendly officers appeared to speak English, but further investigations revealed that Japanese Headquarters at Lahat about 140 miles southwest of Palembang might know something about the nurses; there was also an airstrip at Lahat that might be serviceable. Madsen returned to Singapore with a group of very weak male POWs from a camp at Palembang and provided information that staff of Repatriation of Allied Prisoners of War and Internees required. He was to return the next day, collect Chandler and Windsor and continue on to Lahat if the nurses had been found. Lennard, Flight Officer K. Brown and Major Windsor were to proceed to Lahat. In an account of the mission Windsor wrote, "Just before leaving I was ordered by Lieutenant-Colonel Hayes to remain in Palembang as he considered there was no need for unnecessary speed in contacting the nurses. I obeyed the order, but insisted that the other two be allowed to go, the excuse being that the co-pilot [Brown] had to ascertain the particulars of the Lahat Airfield."[43]

Lennard and Brown arrived in Lahat that night and discovered that the nurses were at Loebok Linggau some eighty miles away. The Lahat airstrip was found suitable to accommodate a Dakota aircraft and the information was phoned back to Palembang and a phone call made to the women's camp near Loebok Linggau. Brown set off by road, which they were warned was impassable, and Lennard by rail, although the Japanese were not sure this was open.

The women at the internment camp had not known that the camp had a telephone and the excitement generated by the news of release created a fervour of activity. After selfishly guarding all food and anything useful they suddenly enjoyed the pleasure of giving. The news spread, the nurses made their farewells and had an enormous party with the Charitas nuns who sang a Dutch farewell to which the nurses replied. Simons wrote, "I made a round of calls, finding lots of difficulty in saying casual words of farewell to the many with whom we had shared intimately the ups and downs of internment, but I was glad of the chance for many of my friends to write letters to be posted in civilisation." The first group left about 4.30 a.m. for the station in open Japanese trucks. It was pouring rain but this dismal trip had none of the gloomy overtones of previous journeys. "As we climbed aboard, there stood Seki against the wire. Silently watching our departure, but apart from an occasional flippant or ribald comment, the Jap captain was ignored."[44] One guard turned to Trotter and said, "You might've won the war but we'll get Australia yet."

Lennard met the drenched first group and directed them to the station whilst he continued to the camp to collect the other group and find Bullwinkel of whom he took particular care. Lennard had expected to find at the most ten nurses but instead there were twenty-four, as well as thirty-six British women whom Mrs Hinch asked him to take. Halfway back to the station Brown arrived after repeated difficulties with cars on jungle roads and bad washaways. Brown reported soon after: "I visited the camp where these women were imprisoned and although I didn't see their barracks, the smell of the camp area was an indication of the conditions under which they had to live. I also met the Camp

Commandant who had been master and I have never set eyes on a more ruthless man. Needless to say we were the most welcome guests these poor souls had seen for many a day and they did not fail to show it." Lennard and Brown had fitted the train with mattresses, sheets, blankets and pillows at Lahat. They became nurses and news reporters for the women.

Lennard and Brown reported with pride that the Australian Army nurses had dressed in their rags of uniforms and, looking terrible and smelling worse, had walked onto the train. Lennard recalled:

> Some were suffering badly from beri-beri. Their knees and legs were hopelessly swollen (a sure sign of beri-beri), and all they could do was shuffle towards the carriages. Their bloated knees just wouldn't move and if they did make an effort to walk normally the pain from beri-beri would be intense. Some were little more than skeletons. One had lost six stone in weight. Their skin was yellow. Yet their determination to get onto the train without help was silently evident, or, so I felt — they smiled at me in appreciation.

Lennard started forward to assist but did not: "You started to go forward to help them . . . and then suddenly stopped. You felt that even that small assistance might be resented . . . that they could manage. Hadn't they done so for four years . . . in a filthy Jap POW camp?"

The train driver would not leave until 8.00 a.m., his normal departure time. "By eight o'clock, one of the Dutch paratroopers who was still with us had raided the station's refreshment booth (paying the bill!) and we were seated in the train munching cakes, this time with the window shutters wide open in defiant memory of our last trip by train."[45] They left Loebok Linggau station amidst the cheers of their own men and "the most horrible expressions of hatred" on the faces of Japanese.[46] They arrived in Lahat at midday; the Japanese provided food and on Lennard's instructions erected sixty beds in case the women had to stay the night if the plane did not arrive. The twenty-four Army nurses and seven stretcher cases were taken to Lahat airstrip where they waited until the plane arrived late that afternoon, delayed because it had blown a tyre on landing at Palembang. Colonel Sage and her assistant Sister J.E. Floyd, who had been a member of the 2/10th AGH but had escaped on the *Empire Star*, were on board. Sage wrote of this meeting in her official report: "As we stepped out of the plane we were thrilled to see twenty-four sisters in their grey cotton uniforms, each wearing the rising sun badge, well, the meeting was one too difficult for me to describe and the occasion the fulfilment of a desire cherished over the years since the fall of Singapore."[47]

The appearance of these two women, one a new Matron-in-Chief and both dressed in grey slacks in place of the former dress, was a great shock to the nurses. "We realized once more how out of date we were standing there in our forlorn uniforms patched with bits and pieces."[48] Trotter's response to the slacks was "What's the Army coming to!" Temporarily some of the nurses wondered how they were going to cope and were not sure whether they wanted to return to civilization.

Reunions were fraught with joy, tears and amazement. Details of the Banka Island massacre had been given to Chandler and Windsor in Palembang by an Australian serviceman, Lieutenant Bull, who had an eyewitness account, śo the depleted numbers were not a shock when they arrived in Lahat, but the remaining twenty-four survivors still had to explain the absence of the eight who were dead. Chandler was astounded by her friend Trotter's weight loss and did not recognize another of her friends from training days, Tweddell, who had been about eleven stone and now was below five stone. Chandler was warned before she left Singapore that if she met Bullwinkel she should not mention her name. Chandler remembered, "Eventually I came to a tall fair haired nurse with her hair cut in a kind of 'Eton crop'. She had the brightest of smiles and seemed to be one of the 'healthiest' of the nurses . . . I was astonished that she seemed to be as well as she looked . . . it was amazing that having suffered as one of the party of nurses at Banka Island, survived being shot, she was such a bright personality."[49] The support of protective colleagues had done much to help Bullwinkel retain a direct manner and an ability to speak of the atrocity. The plane, normally equipped to carry twenty-two, carried thirty-seven, including the stowaway whose wife had died during captivity, but excluding Sage, Floyd and Windsor who remained to care for the other internees. Madsen landed safely in Singapore, with a blown tyre, on 16 September 1945, the day after the search had started.

Readjustment

The Australian Army nurses arrived in Singapore to a bewildering reception. Filthy, excited and tired, most wore the shabby remains of their uniforms that they had salvaged. Pressmen, photographers, Red Cross helpers and wellwishers overwhelmed them with questions, cups of tea in China cups and saucers which they had forgotten how to use, cigarettes and soap. Lennard released his "scoop" and went to bed, Chandler returned to her quarters and cried, physically and emotionally drained, and the twenty-four survivors returned to St Patrick's School, the former home of the 2/13th AGH nurses, and moved into separate, private quarters. There was almost a riot when they arrived as male patients jumped out of bed and yelled abuse and threats at the Japanese for the condition of the women. The Banka Island massacre story was released. The *Courier-Mail* expressed the prevailing feeling in its editorial on 18 September 1945:

> The massacre of 21 Australian nursing sisters is one of the most horrifying stories of Japanese savagery. These devoted women had survived the sinking of the ship which was taking them from Singapore. They had every claim upon the pity of the

enemy when they were cast up helpless on shore. They with most other survivors were done to death on the spot by disciplined Japanese soldiers. Neither the blood lust and confusion of battle nor the panic of fear mitigated this appalling crime.[50]

Bullwinkel's survival made sensational press and is still the most often quoted story of the female POWs. Some of the other POWs have slightly resented the disbelieving remarks of those who had only heard of Bullwinkel's experience and were unaware that altogether twenty-four Army nurses survived Sumatra.

In his eagerness to print the story Dunstan immediately telegraphed complete lists of those recovered, killed or missing in 1942 and the names of the eight who died in captivity. For most of the parents, radio broadcasts were the first conclusive news of their daughters. Although the relatives of those who were presumed dead in 1942 had been informed to that effect, the next-of-kin of those who died during captivity had not.[51] The Japanese had not transmitted the names and the newspaper reports were the first written information received by the relatives and Land Headquarters of their deaths. When the nurses returned to Australia some of these parents brought gifts and came to hear of their daughters. Hannah, as sole survivor of the 2/4th CCS, spent a considerable amount of time with these mothers.

The Press coverage during their stay in Singapore had an alarming effect on relatives and friends in Australia. Simons wrote:

None of us realised how shocking our appearance was to others. We were a bit incensed at what we thought were highly exaggerated stories in the local press on our appearance. So when we were invited to broadcast to Australia and be photographed for home consumption, I said, "Come on girls! This is our chance to show the folk back home how well we look."

It was one of those photos published in Australia which friends begged my father to hide from mother, who was already suffering from the earlier reports of our condition. We must still have looked pretty grim, though by this time we had put on quite a bit of weight.

If they had not been released at least five of the nurses would not have survived much longer.[52]

The nurses' homecoming was delayed until they were in better physical condition. They were cleaned, fed at regular intervals, well nursed and given priority dental treatment. They were given adequate vitamin tablets and a generous protein diet but they were ravenously hungry and some became distended and uncomfortable in the abdomen, which was remedied by a reduction of food intake.[53] Fourteen had scabies which responded to treatment and five had muscular wasting that improved with physiotherapy.[54] Betty Jeffrey was the only tuberculosis victim among the Sumatran prisoners and was hospitalized in Australia for two years; she considered her real problem was dysentery, which they did not treat, and which plagued all the survivors, and still continues to plague some. They gained weight and by the time they left Singapore all but six were back to their weight before capture, and of those six only two were two stone underweight.[55] Immediate postwar surgical operations were often too risky to perform. Their relatives were shocked at their appearance.

The staff and male patients in the 2/14th AGH made every effort to make the nurses as comfortable and happy as possible; some of their friends who belonged to the 2/10th AGH and 2/13th AGH were now members of this hospital. Jeffrey wrote, "Our welcome at this hospital was wonderful. We were very soon surrounded by the familiar faces of the nurses we knew so well, but not one of us could remember their names!" They also encountered this problem when they got back to Australia. The 2/14th AGH nurses decorated their rooms and together with the Red Cross supplied them with items they had gone without for nearly four years: towels, clothes, pyjamas, slippers, shoes, brushes, combs and other gifts including beauty products. The officers and men of the 8th Division and other visitors brought them gifts and news. The nurses compared notes with the men who had been in Changi and found that their experiences were similar. The women improved enough physically to go shopping. The amounts of money given to released POWs were small despite large paybook credits.[56] "Shortie warned Sister Glover, our escort on a shopping expedition to keep an eye on us — we had grown very light fingered since our last visit to Singapore."[57] Gracie Fields gave a concert at the POW Reception Centre at Changi and they saw *Donald Duck*. The nurses gave a sherry party for the staff of the 2/14th AGH and some of their rescue team but they were sent to bed before it finished.

The nurses sent a broadcast to Australia, received recently written cables and letters and wrote home. The next-of-kin of the nurses were also sent the following message by the Commander of 2 Australian Reception Group in Singapore: "For peace of mind of

151

relatives of 24 sisters recovered and now in 2/14th AGH all well cared for and happy and making very good progress. None were molested by the Japanese. This information supplied by Matron-in-Charge who returned with them from Sumatra and assured me of this fact."[58] Colonel Sage gave the nurses talks on the activities of the AANS during the war and looked after their welfare. Jeffrey mused, "It is rather fun to be called 'girls' again, when most of us felt like old hags." Colonel Sage enplaned on 24 September 1945 but her greatest disappointment was that, despite special preparations, military clothing had not arrived for the nurses.[59] Ironically, the nurses arrived back in Australia in borrowed uniforms.

The Australian reception for the nurses from Japan and Sumatra was enthusiastic. Relatives and friends greeted the nurses who returned from Singapore on 5 October 1945 on the hospital ship *Manunda* which called at Perth (18 October 1945), Melbourne (24 October 1945) and Sydney (26 October 1945). Members of the civilian nursing profession, including the President of the Royal Victorian College of Nursing, Miss J. Bell, were among those who greeted the nurses in Melbourne with flowers and sweets. They were given flowers, fruit, chocolate and presents from organizations and individuals. Staff Nurse Keast said:

My first letter home which was a disgrace, from Manila, said for my first meal I want roast pork and steamed date pudding. I'm writing home to my mother and father having not written all those years but you see that's all we thought about and talked about! My family said we never talked to them at all, all we talked about was food. I said we knew you were there . . .

Anyway this came in the local paper and then eventually all the papers and the Minister for Agriculture was a Wagga man and he had pigs . . . so he rang my father and said "I'm sending you a sucking pig as soon as your daughter comes home." It was brought up in Parliament about him doing that . . . You couldn't buy dates which I didn't know and a woman from Perth sent my mother three dates and she got dates from all over Australia . . . I wouldn't know how many turkeys were given to us. Everything you could think of in the way of food was sent to our house . . . Hundreds of coupons (food, clothing, petrol) came into the house . . . from people we had never heard of and never seen.

The women from Queensland travelled by train from Sydney to Brisbane and at stations throughout the journey people rushed out with gifts or to wave — Blanch received a bowl of strawberries. The hospitals were bedecked with flowers. In Brisbane special cars took them from the station to Yeronga Hospital where the 4th Australian Armoured Brigade Band played "We're better off home". A newspaper reported, " 'It is like a dream being in Australia at last,' said Sister Trotter of Queensland, who had been the camp's 'hair-dresser' and responsible for the neat appearance of their hair. 'Even on the trip home we expected to wake up and find ourselves back in Sumatra,' she added.'[60] Years later they still have nightmares of captivity.

The nurses were admitted to hospital and given twenty-eight days' leave when they were well enough. Miss Jeffrey said:

The thing that brought me back to normal life, from POW to home life, was that I was allowed to go home the first night . . . In the morning I got up and we'd all been given a gorgeous pale blue box of face make-up . . . it was marvellous! I was putting

153

it on, well I hadn't played with cosmetics for five years. I'd put some powder on my nose and spilled a bit on the dressing table. I went straight out to the kitchen to the cupboard where Mum used to keep the dusters and there were the dusters . . . I thought that's right I'm home. Both my parents were there, my home was there and the duster was in the right cupboard!

Others were not so fortunate. Parents and close relatives of some of the POWs had died. One girl returned to news of her mother's death and a new family house which was in contrast to the memories of "home" that had sustained her, like the others, through captivity. They were home but not physically or mentally fit for normal civilian life.

Captivity had deprived these women of the things they most wanted: family and friends, freedom and privacy, food, water, clothing and comfortable conditions. They could not, however, immediately adapt to normal life. Upon release the survivors from Sumatra ranged in age from twenty-nine to forty-one and those who were in Japan from thirty to thirty-six. A wide range of complaints were suffered by those who had been in captivity, particularly those in Sumatra: malaria, beri-beri, arthritis, gall bladder and liver complaints, thyroid complaints (manifested years later), tinea and anxiety. After the twenty-eight days' leave they were readmitted for medical assessment. The effects of amoebic dysentery and malaria were common complaints necessitating hospitalization. All but two of the nine Queenslanders had long periods of hospitalization and Tweddell spent ten months in hospital. James spent twelve months there, and Whyte was in bed for eight months with polyarthritis exacerbated by the cold in Japan. Callaghan died in March 1954, having never completely responded to treatment for tuberculosis. Some medical experts considered the women imprisoned in Sumatra to be ten years older than their chronological age. Nonetheless, in some cases they are now as fit, if not fitter, and cope better with their complaints than others of their own age who did not undergo these experiences. Ten of the present twenty-four survivors have outlived their husbands.

Characteristic of the time, most of the nurses were discharged on small pensions with full entitlement for treatment of any upset due to an infestation of malaria, beri-beri or amoebic dysentery. Even now, not all the women are on full entitlement pensions although Hannah now Mrs Allgrove has campaigned strongly that all POWs should have automatic full entitlement. At the time of their demobilization they were more interested in being home and "living" rather than worrying about pensions. They were also compensated for loss of equipment by free replacement of all items issued from Army stocks plus up to three pounds for loss of other items of personal property; however, the nurses who were prisoners in Sumatra had not received compensation for their kit as late as February 1948.[61] The Queenslanders in the group, at least, also received one hundred pounds each from the 2nd AIF Nurses' Fund and twenty pounds each from the Lady Mayoress (Mrs Chandler) from a fund established by the *Courier-Mail* to assist the nurses during their rehabilitation. The nurses received their pay for the duration of their captivity; payment was increased if they had been promoted in absentia.

Anderson, Blanch, Bullwinkel, James and Parker received the Associate Royal Red Cross, and the internees in Japan and many of the internees in Sumatra were Mentioned in Dispatches. All but three of the thirty nurses were demobilized during 1946. Bullwinkel gave evidence at the Australian War Crimes Board of Inquiry in 1945 and went to the Tokyo War Trials in 1946. She was demobilized in September 1947. James gave evidence at the Australian War Crimes Board of Inquiry in 1945 and in 1947 Parker also gave evidence. In 1948 Captain Seki was sentenced to fifteen years' imprisonment for his administration of the camps in Sumatra.

For nearly four years these women had relied upon each other when facing any difficulty. Jessie Blanch, now Mrs Eaton-Lee, recalled, "We got out of uniforms as soon as we could." However, "It was fairly easy adjusting back to civilian life — as everyone was so kind — but I did miss my POW friends, and saw them as often as I could." Some families wanted to hear about the experiences and heaped kindness upon them. Hannah (Mrs Allgrove) recalled: "We missed our companions who had sustained us for so long and understood how we felt. Our people nearly killed us with kindness and couldn't see through our eyes at all." Florence Trotter (Mrs Syer) remembered that she found people too light, superficial and frivolous. Families and friends could not understand what they had been through or how they had changed and did not have their common interests. Anderson returned to Grafton where she was treated as an oddity which made her retreat into herself and wish for the security of internment. Some of the nurses did not talk of their experiences and many still do not except to their POW friends. One of the POWs felt her family was more interested in its own wartime problems in Australia than in her experiences.

A few of the nurses married almost immediately; altogether sixteen of the survivors of Sumatra married, eight having children, and five of the six in Japan married, two having children. Some took advantage of the War Service Home Loan Assistance. Nevertheless, they sought each other out and went on trips together whenever possible. They talked about the funny incidents of captivity. Jean Greer, Mrs Pemberton, recollected: "Despite the wonderful welcome it seemed a very lonely time. So much so that we used to try and meet the others from camp for lunch or for drinks after duty every day until we got used to being among civilians and living a different life altogether."[62] The Matron of Anderson's training school came to see her in hospital and offered her a job back on the staff. The hospital allowed her to resume a normal working lifestyle slowly and gave her an interest and a challenge. Trotter convinced Allan & Stark Limited, a Brisbane department store, of the benefits of nursing care in businesses and became their first industrial nurse in 1946. Hannah ran a clinic for the locals on her husband's estate in Malaya. Jeffrey and Bullwinkel travelled Victoria to publicize and raise funds for the Nurses' Memorial Centre which Jeffrey then ran as administrator. Bullwinkel worked at the Repatriation Hospital at Heidelberg and later became Matron of the Fairfield Infectious Diseases Hospital. She has received an MBE, ARRC, ED and the Florence Nightingale Medal (the highest award of the International Red Cross Committee given every two years for services to nursing). She was also appointed to the governing body of the Royal Humane Society of Australasia which assesses the bravery of rescuers being considered for awards. Those who re-entered the workforce, particularly as nurses, were fortunate that their occupation involved mixing with others and having to become familiar with wartime changes in medicine; their profession assisted them in yet another practical way.

For the duration of the war these women had lived as sisters in a family but under unusually stressful conditions. Their rescue diminished all the material desires that had obsessed them during captivity but also provided new challenges quite different from the monotony and simplicity of the years of captivity. Marriage, children, job commitments and living in different states and nations have not erased the bonds that exist between these women. "We have lived and suffered together. Other RSL groups don't like us . . . We are too cliquey . . . but you can't blame us, can you?"[63]

Conclusion

The Australian Army nurses who became POWs were part of an unwanted legacy for Japan resulting from its momentous victory in the East. Subject to the pressures and events of warfare, both groups, in Sumatra and in Japan, experienced similar kinds of unremitting emotional and physical hardship. The internment camps were a new testing-ground for the endurance and fortitude that women can show under demanding circumstances.

The reasoning behind the Japanese treatment of prisoners is a subject in itself. Japan's policy of "Asia for the Asians" meant the removal of Europeans and service personnel. Individual Japanese differed in their attitude but generally all camps suffered shortages of necessities. As supply lines were unable to keep up with Japanese expansion conditions became progressively worse. Japanese cities were bombed and guards' families and friends were killed. Bitterness at the death of innocents is by no means limited to one culture.

In all but a few cases the hatred the POWs felt towards their captors has diminished over the years. At most they dislike or distrust them, but recognize that

Japan is part of Australia's economic life. Before the war the Japanese were an unknown race. Since, some of the women have visited Japan and been impressed by the courtesy and inventiveness of the Japanese. Despite their treatment they do not want to forget the value of the experience. Miss Tweddell wrote, "The comradeship and feeling for each other will remain and if possible we will always help each other." Miss Jean Ashton agreed, "You find out what really matters in life. One can do without material things. Faith, hope, love and the greatest of these is love and companionship and true friends."

An egalitarian spirit pervaded these women's camps that was not always evident in male POW camps.[64] Disciplinary measures implemented by virtue of rank did not occur although the nurses had levels of military seniority. Discipline was a matter of overcoming personal disagreements, not calling upon a senior authority to solve the problem. They counselled each other. The Japanese did not attempt to undermine authority as they did in some of the men's camp; nor were the senior staff unwilling to accept responsibility.[65]

The bond of friendship that these women developed merits the term "mateship". This ideal, fostered by the official historian of the First World War, C.E.W. Bean, has come to be symbolic of Australian male associations particularly during wartime, but in this instance it was also displayed by Army nurses in captivity. Their prewar friendships intensified under conditions of deprivation. The differences of opinion and disagreements during captivity were unimportant compared to the unifying spirit of these women and the problem of surviving another day.

The title of the service to which they belonged, the Australian Army Nursing Service, expressed the sense of identity the nurses exhibited. These women accepted that they were Australians caught by the Japanese; patriotism at an individual level existed and they were determined to outwit their captors. The Army nurses reacted in a similar manner to captivity as did civilian internees willing to participate in group activities, but these Australian Army nurses had a particular Australian military identity as well as the common bond of nursing which created forceful ties. The title "Army Nurses", was dropped in Sumatra and they were known as "Australian Nurses", but they never lost consciousness of their role. Throughout captivity they retained their loyalties to Australia and their military units despite the friendships they made outside these groupings. Since the nurses' return from Japan they have maintained their military connections although they have lost contact with the civilians. These women left home and family to do something useful for their country; the hostilities they encountered turned friends into family. Their role as Army nurses gave them pride in themselves as well as their country.

The thirty-eight Australian Army nurses who became POWs during World War Two exhibited strength, courage, cohesion and a sense of identity that overcame differences in personalities. They positively and effectively combated the adverse circumstances that sorely tried their survival measures. The horrors, the sadness and the humour of captivity are now memories, but the bonds of friendship remain. These women survived primitive lifestyles and saw the essence of human nature. They gained in tolerance, understanding, patience and forbearance and acquired through their experience an enhanced view of the value of the concepts of comradeship and community life. They have a profound humility in being alive. As Miss Betty Jeffrey said, "It was rough on us . . . but everybody had a bad war."

Notes

1. *History of AANS 1939–1945*, p. 1, 509/1/1, Australian War Memorial, Canberra.
2. T. Hamilton, *Soldier Surgeon in Malaya* (Sydney: Angus & Robertson, 1957), p. 13.
3. Ibid.
4. A.S. Walker et al., *Medical Services of the RAN and RAAF with a section on Women in the Army Medical Services* (Canberra: Australian War Memorial, 1961), p. 451.
5. [2/10th AGH nurse], "Malaya", *Lest We Forget*, Commemorative Booklet for the *Centaur* War Memorial Fund (1944), pp. 16-18.
6. S/N A.B. Jeffrey, Personal Diary, Book 1, p. 1, 3 DRL 1857, Australian War Memorial, Canberra.
7. J.J. Eaton-Lee (Blanch), "Three Years as a White Coolie", *Grey and Scarlet* 3 (1981): 11.
8. J.E. Simons, *While History Passed* (Melbourne: William Heinemann, 1954), p. 21.
9. Ibid., p. 22.
10. Statement by VFX 61330 Sister V. Bullwinkel, p. 2, 2/14th AGH War Diary, Part 2, Written Records 1939-45, 11/2/14, Australian War Memorial, Canberra.
11. Statement by Sister N.G. James to the Australian War Crimes Board of Inquiry, 1 November 1945, p. 2, Written Records 1939-45, 1010/4/78, Australian War Memorial, Canberra.
12. Jeffrey, Personal Diary, March 1942, Bk. 1.
13. H. Nelson, *Prisoners of War, Australians Under Nippon* (Sydney: ABC Enterprises, 1985), p. 79.
14. Jeffrey, Personal Diary, Bk. 2.
15. B. Jeffrey, *White Coolies* (Sydney: Angus & Robertson, 1954), p. 51.
16. Ibid., p. 52.
17. Jeffrey, Personal Diary, December 1942, Bk. 2.

18. Ibid., January 1943.
19. Simons, *While History Passed*, pp. 61-62.
20. [J.H. Beith], *One Hundred Years of Army Nursing* (London: Cassell and Co., 1953), p. 273.
21. L. Warner and J. Sandilands, *Women Beyond the Wire: A Story of Prisoners of the Japanese 1942–45* (London: Michael Joseph, 1982), p. 181.
22. Medical Report "A", p. 27, 11/2/14, Australian War Memorial, Canberra.
23. [Beith], *One Hundred Years of Army Nursing*, p. 273.
24. Jeffrey, *White Coolies*, p. 145.
25. J. Smyth, *The Will to Live: The Story of Dame Margot Turner OBE, RRC* (London: Cassell, 1970), p. 110.
26. Jeffrey, Personal Diary, 9 January 1945, Bk. 3.
27. Statement by Sister N.G. James, p. 11, MP742, 336/1/1289, Australian Archives, Melbourne.
28. Jeffrey, *White Coolies*, p. 188.
29. G.F. Jacobs, *Prelude To The Monsoon* (Cape Town: Purnell, 1965), p. 134.
30. Ibid., p. 136.
31. Mrs Bignell, *Yokohama*, Personal Collection, Mrs Morris-Yates, NSW.
32. *Australian Women's Weekly*, 29 September 1945, p. 10.
33. Cable 1027 from Geneva re IRCC Delegates Visit to Kanagawa Civil Internee Camp no. 2, Totsuka, Yokohama, on 23 August 1945, p. 1, CRS A 816, 37/301/277A, Australian Archives, Canberra.
34. Jean M. McLellan, Personal Diary, January 1942-3 September 1945, Personal Collection, Mrs J.M. Harwood (McLellan), Qld.
35. J. Newman Morris, *The Story of the Red Cross and Prisoners of War in Japanese Hands* (Melbourne, 1944), Mitchell Library, Sydney.
36. High Commissioner's Office (London) cablegram to Prime Minister's Department, 28 December 1943, MP 1217, Box 672, Australian Archives, Canberra.
37. Report of Interrogation of Seventy-eight AIF POWs Rescued by Submarine in China Sea on 15 September 1944, p. 34, MP 729/8, 44/431/53, Australian Archives, Melbourne.
38. B. Maddock (Chandler), "Flight Sister", unpublished book, Personal Collection, Mrs Maddock, Qld, 1983, p. 172.
39. Cable 1027 from Geneva re IRCC Delegates Visit to Totsuka, Yokohama, 23 August 1945, p. 1.
40. Ibid.
41. Walker et al., *Medical Services of RAN and RAAF*, p. 455.
42. Maddock, "Flight Sister", p. 155.
43. Major H.M. Windsor, 2/14th AGH, an account of the evacuation of AANS personnel, Australian servicemen and civilian internees from Palembang, Lahat, Loebok Linggau and Belalau Prison Camp in Sumatra, p. 1, MP 742, 336/1/1289, Australian Archives, Melbourne.
44. Simons, *While History Passed*, p. 116.

45. Ibid., p. 117.
46. Jeffrey, *White Coolies*, p. 198.
47. Colonel A.M. Sage, Report on the Tour of Duty to Sumatra, p. 1, MP 742, 336/1/1289, Australian Archives, Melbourne.
48. Jeffrey, *White Coolies*, p. 198.
49. Maddock, "Flight Sister", p. 177.
50. *Courier-Mail*, 18 September 1945, p. 2.
51. Recovery of 24 Members of the AANS from Japanese, Department of Army Minute Paper, 11 October 1945, p. 1, MP 742, 336/1/1289, Australian Archives, Melbourne. Ms Rita Dunstan, who is researching A.E. Dunstan's life story, questions this account and contends she knows of no basis for the Army Minute Paper singling out her brother.
52. Medical Report "A", p. 27, 11/2/14, Australian War Memorial, Canberra.
53. Ibid., p. 28.
54. Ibid.
55. Ibid.
56. 2/14th AGH War Diary, p. 25, 11/2/14, Pt. 1, Australian War Memorial, Canberra.
57. Simons, *While History Passed*, p. 123.
58. Commander 2 Australian POW Reception Group to Adjutant-General, October 1945, point 5, MP 742, 336/1/1289, Australian Archives, Melbourne.
59. 2/14th AGH War Diary, 24 September 1945.
60. "Nurses Return", undated newspaper clipping, Personal Collection, Mrs Syer, Qld.
61. *Commonwealth Parliamentary Debates*, 195, 20 November 1947, p. 2429.
62. Warner and Sandilands, *Women Beyond the Wire*, p. 267.
63. Eaton-Lee, "Three Years as a White Coolie", p. 13.
64. H. Nelson, "Travelling in Memories: Australian prisoners of the Japanese, forty years after the Fall of Singapore", *Journal of the Australian War Memorial* 3 (1983): 19.
65. O. Lindsay, "The Recovery of Prisoners of War and Civilian Internees from Japan", *Defence Force Journal* 28 (1981): 51.

References

For further information please consult the extensive bibliography in my Honours thesis, *Australian Army Nurses in Japanese Captivity 1942–1945*, held by the History Department, University of Queensland.

Bullwinkel, Sister V. Statement to the Australia War Crimes Board of Inquiry, 29 October 1945. 1010/4/24, Australia War Memorial, Canberra.

Bullwinkel, Sister V. Statement in The Procedures for the International Military Tribunal of the Far East 1947–48. Micro. 3949, University of Queensland, Brisbane.

James, Sister N.G. Statement to the Australian War Crimes Board of Inquiry, 1 November 1945. 1010/4/78, Australian War Memorial, Canberra.

Jeffrey, Staff Nurse A.B. Personal Diary. 3 DRL 1857, Australian War Memorial, Canberra.

McLellan, Jean M. Personal Diary, 4 January 1942–3 September 1945. Personal Collection Mrs J.M. Harwood (McLellan), Brisbane, Qld.

Medical Points of Interest Arising from the Internment of Members of AANS in Sumatra. Appendix "A", 2/14th AGH War Diary, p. 25, Pt. 1, 11/2/14, Australian War Memorial, Canberra.

Personal communications with nurses who were POWs, held by the author.

Clarence, M. *Yield Not To The Wind*. Sydney: Management Development Publishers, 1982.

Jeffrey, B. *White Coolies*. Sydney: Angus & Robertson, 1954, 1975.

Simons, J.E. *While History Passed: The Story of the Australian Nurses who were prisoners of the Japanese for three and a half years*. Melbourne: William Heinemann, 1954. Reprinted as *In Japanese Hands: Australian Nurses as POWs*, 1985.

Warner, L. and Sandilands, J. *Women Beyond the Wire: A Story of Prisoners of the Japanese 1942–45*. London: Michael Joseph, 1982.

Nurses Captured by the Japanese

NFX180285   Anderson, Staff Nurse Marjory J., Australian Army Nursing Service

NFX180289   Callaghan, Staff Nurse Eileen M., Australian Army Nursing Service

NFX180290   Cullen, Staff Nurse Mavis C., Australian Army Nursing Service

NFX180286   Keast, Staff Nurse Daisy C. (Tootie), Australian Army Nursing Service

NFX180287   Parker, Sister Kathleen I.A. (Kay), Australian Army Nursing Service

NFX180288   Whyte, Staff Nurse Lorna M., Australian Army Nursing Service

SFX13548   Ashton, Sister Carrie Jean, 2/13th AGH

NFX70528   Blake, Staff Nurse Kathleen C., 2/10th AGH

QFX19074   Blanch, Staff Nurse Jessie J., 2/10th AGH

VFX61330   Bullwinkel, Staff Nurse Vivian, 2/13th AGH

NFX76282	Clancy, Staff Nurse Veronica A., 2/13th AGH
NFX70498	Davis, Sister Winnie M., 2/10th AGH
QFX19071	Delforce, Staff Nurse Cecilia M., 2/10th AGH
NFX70499	Doyle, Sister Jess G., 2/10th AGH
VFX39351	Freeman, Staff Nurse Rubina D., 2/10th AGH
TFX2183	Gardam, Staff Nurse Dorothy S., 2/4th CCS
NFX70937	Greer, Staff Nurse Jean K., 2/10th AGH
NFX70493	Gunther, Staff Nurse Janet P., 2/10th AGH
SFX10595	Hannah, Sister Ellen Mavis, 2/4th CCS
WFX11172	Harper, Staff Nurse Iole, 2/13th AGH
QFX22714	Hempsted, Sister Pauline B., 2/13th AGH
VFX61331	Hughes, Staff Nurse Gladys L., 2/13th AGH
VFX39347	James, Sister Nesta G., 2/10th AGH
VFX53059	Jeffrey, Staff Nurse Agnes Betty, 2/10th AGH
QFX22822	McElnea, Staff Nurse Violet I., 2/13th AGH
QFX19068	Mittelheuser, Sister Pearl B., 2/10th AGH
QFX22816	Muir, Staff Nurse Sylvia J. M., 2/13th AGH
VFX58783	Oram, Staff Nurse Wilma E. F., 2/13th AGH
QFX19073	Oxley, Staff Nurse Christian S. M., 2/10th AGH

TFX6012	Raymont, Staff Nurse Wilhelmina R., 2/4th CCS
QFX22911	Short, Staff Nurse Eileen M., 2/13th AGH
TFX6023	Simons, Staff Nurse Jessie E., 2/13th AGH
VFX48842	Singleton, Staff Nurse Irene A., 2/10th AGH
QFX22819	Smith, Staff Nurse Valrie E., 2/13th AGH
WFX11105	Syer, Staff Nurse Ada C., 2/10th AGH
QFX19077	Trotter, Staff Nurse Florence E., 2/10th AGH
QFX19070	Tweddell, Staff Nurse Joyce, 2/10th AGH
VFX53060	Woodbridge, Staff Nurse Beryl, 2/10th AGH

These ranks were taken from Army records and were correct at the beginning of the war. A number of the Staff Nurses were promoted to Sister during and after the war.

Index

172